CHRISTIAN FAMILIES
IN THE REAL WORLD

CHRISTIAN FAMILIES IN THE REAL WORLD

Reflections on a Spirituality for the Domestic Church

Mitch and Kathy Finley

THE THOMAS MORE PRESS
Chicago, Illinois

ISBN 0-88347-163-9

CONTENTS

DEDICATION

To the Most Reverend Bernard J. Topel, retired bishop of the Diocese of Spokane, Washington, whose far-sighted vision, love for the gospel, and understanding of the critical importance of family ministry to the future of the church inspired him to take the financial and other risks necessary to open a diocesan Family Life Office in 1972.

FOREWORD

UNFORTUNATELY much of what passes for family spirituality at the present time is as pertinent to the typical American Catholic family as is the monastic spirituality depicted so sharply in Umberto Eco's *The Name of the Rose.* Whether produced by the Vatican or by episcopal conferences or family life "movements" or "religious educators," the so-called family spirituality literature is almost entirely aprioristic. It seeks to impose on the contemporary American family the ideological concerns of the past or the present without any sensitivity to the actual situations in which modern families live.

This literature knows the answers to the family's questions without bothering to listen to the questions.

Such an attitude pervaded the disastrous synod on the family a couple of years ago. A group of men who did not have families of their own and who had not bothered to do research about the condition of the contemporary family pontificated at great length about the problems of family life and offered detailed and elaborate recommendations of how the family ought to live.

They were so blind to their own folly as not to realize what a laughing stock they had made of themselves.

The typical "intervention" at the Synod seemed to assume a model of family life that might have been typical of the bourgeois family in southern European countries in the middle of the last century—the husband and wife do not sleep together because they are honoring the church's teaching on contraception (the

7

ideal family, it seems, is one in which sex has stopped long ago), the wife spends her time at home taking care of the children, and the wife and children wait quietly and eagerly for their marching orders from husband and father.

Thus do the Lords Spiritual advise the family.

And if one is dubious about them, one can turn to the "religious educators" and the "peace and justice" crowd who apparently want to turn the family into a junior grade marxist revolutionary cell, grimly determined to expiate for its own victimization of the third world (and everyone else's too.)

Against the background of trash from the right and the left, the work of Mitch and Kathy Finley shines very brightly indeed. They recognize the pluralism of situations in which families find themselves. They do not attempt to impose any apriori paradigms on their readers. They are blessedly free of the jargon and the doctrinaire perspectives which dominate so much current Catholic literature. And they are neither obsessed by sex nor afraid to mention it.

And they clearly understand what family life is like from the inside. They sense the opportunities and the dangers, the hopes and the failures, the deaths and rebirths which are part of every day existence in real families. Their work represents one of the few honest and able attempts to develop a wisdom about family life. May many others benefit from their wisdom and be inspired to make their own contribution.

Andrew M. Greeley

The family was ordained of God. . .it was
before the church, or rather the first
form of the church on earth.

Pope Leo XIII

Introduction

THE FAMILY IS CHURCH

AN important insight in the teachings of the Second Vatican Council has been neglected by virtually every major theologian whose subject has been the theology of the church. Little if any awareness is found in their writings of the value of the conciliar teaching that the family constitutes "the domestic church." Theologians tend to either ignore this idea, or mention it only in passing with a very limited understanding of its implications for both families and the church as a whole.

As Bishop J. Francis Stafford, of the Diocese of Memphis, Tennessee, has observed: "Since the Council of Trent (1545-63) the church has lost a family dimension in its understanding of religious life...We have now relegated most of our religious life to the parish, to the detriment of the families." Bishop Stafford adds: "Very few persons who are studying theology professionally today give any attention to the religious mysteries of marriage and family life."

But those who belong to families intuitively realize that their faith makes little sense apart from what goes on in the daily experience of family relationships. Together with those who work closely with families, they know that the family—in its various forms—is "the foundational church" (a term coined by theologian David M. Thomas). It is within the family that the foundational experiences of the Christian life happen best, for both children and adults. For most people, it is within the fabric of family life that faith becomes real.

Still, when Vatican II called the family "the domestic

11

church," this was nothing original. The conviction that
the family is the most basic religious community pre-
dates the gospel. In Jewish tradition the home—not the
synagogue—is the center of religious life. And in
distinctively Christian terms, the basic New Testament
concept of church is reflected in the words of Jesus:
"Where two or three are gathered together in my name,
there am I in their midst." Whatever else these words
describe, they clearly apply to the Christian family.

When the earliest Christians were banned from the
synagogue, they naturally gravitated to private homes.
By the late fourth century, St. John Chrysostom (in his
sermons on the book of Genesis and in his commentary
on the Epistle to the Ephesians) was writing of the family as *ecclesia* (the Greek theological term for "church").
Only once did John Chrysostom use the diminutive
form, *ecclesiola* ("little church"); more often he simply
called the family *ecclesia*—church.

In modern times, Pope Leo XIII wrote: "The family
was ordained of God. . .it was before the church, or
rather the first form of the church on earth."

It is also significant that the Second Vatican Council
decided to discuss the family not in a separate document, but in the context of a central document on the
church.

In the years following the council, Pope Paul VI frequently recalled that the family is the domestic church.
He said that the family is the most basic cell not only of
society, but of the church as well. In his Apostolic Exhortation on Evangelization, Paul VI spelled out in
more detail an important implication of this teaching:
". . .there should be found in every Christian family the
various aspects of the entire church."

The Christian family *is* church. In the course of his homily at the Eucharist which opened the 1980 Synod of Bishops, Pope John Paul II gave his own concise formulation to this teaching when he said that the family is meant to "constitute the church in its fundamental dimension."

Finally, it is also significant that no less a theologian than Bernard Cooke writes in his recent book, *Sacraments and Sacramentality*: "The Christian family is meant to be the most basic instance of Christian community, people bonded together by their shared relationship to the risen Jesus."

All this means that in great part both the local parish and the universal church depend upon families for their fundamental vitality as they strive to make Christ present in the modern world.

Virtually everyone belongs to a family—a domestic church—in some way. Young newly wed couples are a family. Single parent familes are also a true form of domestic church. Older couples whose children have grown, and childless couples, constitute authentic forms of familial and ecclesial life.

Priests and vowed religious go on participating in some way in their extended family of origin. Too, relationships with other priests or religious—whether in a rectory or a religious community house—ideally should constitute for priests and religious a form of family life. Indeed, many founders of religious orders spoke of the need for community life to be modeled after family life.

Single people of any age still belong to their family of origin and almost always have a network of primary relationships which, for them, serves as a continuing experience of family life.

Christian tradition clearly teaches that the family—in its various forms—is an authentic and indispensable form of church. Yet the notion that the family is the most basic cell of ecclesial life has had little impact on the life of the average Catholic. It has had almost no effect on most parishes. Many homilies and lectures have been delivered since Vatican II on the church as People of God and Body of Christ. Now and then a diocese has latched onto the idea of calling the church a "family" at fund-raising time. But only recently have there been efforts to benefit from the ancient teaching that the family is *ecclesia*, the foundational church.

It is time to begin to take seriously the fact that the parish depends for its existence on Christian families and that parish and family are interdependent. In the words of a 1979 statement by the Papal Commission for the Family, "This is the time to present the family as the center of the pastoral reflection of the church."

The first form of church into which an infant is baptized is the church of the family. As so many pastoral theologians remind us today, the baptism of a baby makes little sense apart from daily opportunities for the growing child to experience the Christian life in his or her family relationships.

It is within the family and around the family table that children experience the meaning of Eucharist long before they make their first communion. It is within the fabric of life in the domestic church that child and adult experience the meaning of forgiveness and reconciliation, apart from any officially sacramental celebration of this experience. It is in the family that both adults and children experience the Christian life at its most immediate, where the seeds of faith are planted and cultivated daily.

This book is about a spirituality for families, a spirituality that is suggested by the traditional teaching that the family is *ecclesia*. In particular, this spirituality takes its cues from the words of Paul VI: "There should be found in every Christian family the various aspects of the entire church."

But "spirituality" is one of those time-worn terms which tends to suggest more—and less—than it should. Even today it summons up a split between body and soul, between spirit and flesh, between religious and secular life. Another understanding of "spirituality" is taken for granted here. For the spiritual life actually takes human nature as a cohesive whole and relates it to the Divine Mystery. That is, a spirituality for families refers as much to family conflict as it does to family prayer. It has as much to do with the day in, day out, relationships between family members as it does with the relationship of faith between the family and God.

"Family spirituality" means no more and no less than this: A family's ongoing attempts to live every dimension of its life in communion with the cross and resurrection of Jesus Christ. Yet every family is unique in its spirituality as every family has a personality of its own. In a very real sense, the Smith family will have a Smith spirituality, the Atkinsons an Atkinson spirituality, and the Wilsons a Wilson spirituality. Of course, each of these unique family spiritualities will also share a common spirit through a shared faith in the real presence of Christ who dwells in each family's midst.

This book is based on the conviction that if a family is—in reality and not merely by way of a pious analogy—a genuine form of church, of ecclesial life, then certain principles for a family spirituality and family lifestyle will follow quite naturally.

If a family is *ecclesia,* then it is first of all to be a community, an intimate network of personal relationships. As a Christian community, the family is also to be of service to one another and to those outside the family who have special needs. The family is also to be a community which prays and ritualizes its faith in ways natural to families. Because the spirit and life of the family are guided by the gospel, the family finds itself inclined to adopt attitudes and values which are sometimes counter-cultural. The ways God speaks in the gospel, in the church, and in the events of our times leads families today to a new understanding and awareness of the impact of human sexuality on families and on the family roles of men and women. Single parent families find themselves confronted by unique challenges to be guided and sustained by the Spirit. The domestic church, in its various forms, is called to proclaim the gospel, to be a light on a hilltop and the salt of the earth.

The most basic form of family life is marriage. Therefore, a married couple constitutes the smallest possible expression of ecclesial life, too. In the traditional two parent nuclear family, the married couple is the foundation of the foundational church. And parents, through their special role in families, function in a pastoral as well as a socializing capacity.

Finally, the relationship between the domestic church and the parish is an extremely important one. Each form of ecclesial life depends upon and supports the other.

The following pages present discussions of these topics in the light of their contribution to a family spirituality. The reflections offered here are intended more as a stimulus for unique families to discover their own unique spirituality than as a guide book to be consulted for specific instructions.

In the Foreword to his contemporary classic, *The Affluent Society*, economist John Kenneth Galbraith remarks: "Authorship of any sort is a fantastic indulgence of the ego. It is well, no doubt, to reflect on how much one owes to others."

We would like to express our thanks to the following people: Kay Babcock, for valuable insights into the experience of single parents; Clayton Barbeau, for the inspiration of his life, and of his marriage to his late wife, Myra; Rev. Donald Conroy, for sharing with us his enthusiasm for and vision of family ministry, and for his support, encouragement and friendship; Bob and Dolores DuPont, for their many years of marriage, their beautiful family, and for welcoming us at their table; Rev. Andrew M. Greeley, for the sociological research he and his colleagues have done on Catholic families today, and for generously contributing a Foreword to this book; Hans and Mallene Herzog and the couples who serve in the Marriage Preparation Weekends program of the Diocese of Spokane, for sharing with us their marriages, families, friendship, and for their dedicated example of service to others; Bob and Karen Kopesky, for taking us in when we were "strangers in a strange land," and for showing us what hospitality means; Dan Morris, for inviting us to write a weekly column for our diocesan newspaper, thus affording us opportunities to reflect on many of the themes which appear in this book; Rev. Tom Royce, S.J., for sharing himself so readily with families; David M. Thomas, for some of the key theological principles upon which our reflections are based; the Most Reverend Bernard J. Topel, retired bishop of the Diocese of Spokane, for giving us the opportunity to become involved in family ministry, and for his kind support of our efforts during those years; the entire community of St. Benedict the Moor Parish, Milwaukee, Wisconsin, for showing us what a parish can be; and a special thanks to all the families who have helped us to reflect honestly on a spirituality for real families in the real world.

Chapter 1

THE FAMILY IS A COMMUNITY

IT is not possible to be Christian apart from a community of faith. It is a contradiction of terms to think of being Christian in isolation from others. Even those rare individuals who receive a special religious calling to live as hermits continue to belong to a human and ecclesial community.

This is why the sacrament of baptism is understood today in one very important sense as a sacrament of initiation into the ecclesial community. For to be joined to Christ through baptism is also to be joined to his Body, the People of God. The two cannot be separated.

To say that the family is church is to say that the first form of Christian community in which the person participates is the community of his or her family. In terms borrowed directly from the New Testament tradition, my "neighbor" is first those with whom I live most closely, the other members of my family. These are the "neighbors" Christ commands us to love.

Families are also typically and frequently hot-beds of conflict. It is at times of family conflict that the "enemy" Jesus tells me to love is also a member of my family. The "enemy" is that two-year-old who is driving me to delirium, the teen-ager whose rebellious behavior is carrying me to the brink of an ulcer, or my spouse who continues to squeeze the toothpaste in the middle of the tube, even after all these years.

As a member of a family/domestic church, I respond to my Christian vocation by a dedication to "building community" within the family to which I belong. If my family is the place where I participate in the most fundamental ways in Christian community life, then it is vital for the family as a whole to make a firm commitment to "love one another"—to actively stay in touch with one another and care for one another. This means that as a family we care enough to be there regularly for one another for no other reason than the fact that we are a family.

The domestic church is a community of baptized Christians. Part of membership in this church-community is the willingness—indeed, the enthusiasm—to make time for each other regulariy.

In his lectures, author and family counselor Clayton C. Barbeau makes the point that time is not found; I do not discover ten minutes lying on the sidewalk one day, much as I might come upon a dime someone has dropped by accident. Rather, time is made; I make the time to spend on those activities and interests that are of greatest value to me. I have only a certain amount of time in my day, in my week—in my life. I must take responsibility for deciding how I will use my time.

This is precisely what Christian families must do if they are to build up their relationships with one another and thus build up the Body of Christ in their midst. There must be a setting of priorities, with time given to family relationships very near the top of the list. The domestic church community has no choice in today's hectic world but to sacrifice some less important interests and activities outside the family circle in order to allow for regular time together.

The calendar of a typical Christian family tends to be filled with commitments to many activities and organizations which, rather than bringing the family together, fragment it yet further. Most of these involvements are with "good" and "worthy" causes: parish social activities, day-care co-ops, parish educational programs, school-related sports programs, civic organizations that depend on volunteer help, Scouting programs. . . .The list is endless.

A renewed awareness of the importance of nourishing family relationships demands that the Christian family make sacrifices as an expression of love. No one—and no family—can participate in all the worthwhile or attractive opportunities for involvement outside the family that naturally come along. When I decide to do this, it means I cannot do that. If staying in touch with one another and staying close to one another's lives is the high value that it must be for the Christian family today, then something on the calendar will have to go—for all members of the family. Involvement in one sport at school instead of two; joining the school newspaper staff and skipping the spring drama production; helping out with the Cub Scouts, but saying "sorry" to the parish fund drive. Perhaps there will be a need for the whole family to live with the sacrifices necessary because Dad must say no to a promotion which would bring in more money, but would require him to spend more time away from the family.

Of course, once the family has decided to make the time to be together regularly, there are many ways to spend this time. Some families designate one night a week as Family Night. Not a few families get into the Family Nights habit by trying it for a month or six weeks (perhaps during Lent) just to see how it goes. All agree to keep this night free from other involvements. Everyone stays home—or we all go together to some shared activity outside the home. This can be a time for simple forms of shared prayer, time to talk about how each person's life is going, time for some laughter, time to simply enjoy one another. The point is that the family decides on some mutually agreeable way to be together regularly, to overcome the fragmentation which tends to afflict families today. This is the time to make some effort toward keeping family relationships intimate rather than allowing them to become superficial.

Family times together are times for "preventive maintenance." We spend a couple of hours preventing "generation gaps." We do what we can to prevent our house from becoming little more than a "refueling station" and a place to sleep. We take positive steps to love one another in ways that can be felt.

An appointment calendar distributed by the advertising department of a newspaper has little "blurbs" scattered throughout its pages—motivational messages from the newspaper which are intended to offer the wisdom of the marketplace to prospective purchasers of advertising space. One bit of commercial wisdom states: "You can get more buying action when you get your advertising message into the family circle."

From the perspective of the American marketplace, the family is first of all a gathering of consumers, and some of the "market value" of the family arises precisely from the individual's membership in a family. Families are where most babies live, and babies are a multi-billion-dollar-a-year business. Millions of dollars a year are spent on weddings. Much pressure is brought to bear on parents to keep their offspring dressed in a stylish fashion.

Because the American family is typically isolated from other families—usually in every way but geographically—each family must have its own washing machine, lawn mower, ladder, television set, and car. So a family is primarily a market, a buyer of "consumer goods."

The living room of the American family has become, through the presence of television, perhaps *the* primary target for advertising campaigns. It is vital that the Christian family recover its role as the primary molder of the spirit of its members. We are not primarily consumers. Rather, we are persons who need one another more than we need more possessions. It is vital that in a world of strangers the members of a family take the trouble to remain close to one another. This decision will bring a family into conflict with a materialistic value system which proclaims that human happiness and fulfillment are to be found through the buying and accumulation of more and more possessions.

Families will encounter other obstacles in their effort to nourish intimate family relationships. Consider, for example, the secular value of privacy. In our world today, privacy is all but an ultimate value. The more bathrooms in a family's home, the better. Most American homes have two or more television sets; that way, if you don't like what the kids are watching you can avoid conflict by moving to another room and another television set. So now, not only do we not communicate with one another while watching TV, we also watch different programs in different rooms.

The point, of course, is not that multiplying bathrooms or television sets is destructive of family life in itself. The point is that when such facts tend to

characterize our family living arrangments, we need to
be sensitive to their possible negative impact on family
relationships and take counter-measures to prevent
such negative effects.

Another ideal of the American family seems to be for
each family member who is old enough to drive to have
his or her own car; that way no one needs to take anyone
else into account when making plans that require the
use of a car. Again, the goal is to prevent conflict.

If the behavior of many families is any gauge, it
would seem that each member of the family has a right
to eat *what* he or she wants, *when* he or she wants it.
The idea of three family meals at regular times each day
is archaic! The family meal—at least in the evening—is
perhaps the last hold-out for many families as a time to
be together at least once a day. But even the evening
meal as a family time is a rarity for many families. The
family meal is an "endangered species." "After all,"
goes the refrain, "how can parents expect everyone to
be present at the same time for dinner?" Daughter has
tennis practice and Son is on the baseball team! And
besides, Dad is working overtime this month. It seems
that often the schedules are in charge of the family, instead of vice versa.

Perhaps the ultimate travesty of family time is the image of a family gathered around the TV set with dinner
plates on their laps. Together we stare at the Tube,
together we stuff food in our mouths. Probably our
"together" time is punctuated by one-liners hurled at
the program being watched and at one another.
Throughout the entire process (before most of us
stampede in our different directions for the evening)
rarely, if ever, do any human forms of interaction take

place that could not also have occurred between strangers.

I crave human intimacy. But I want my privacy. Intimacy means—among other things—conflict. I don't like conflict; it's too painful. I don't want to deal with the difficulties I will encounter if I really make an effort to *be with* the other members of my family. (Can you imagine the pain of only one bathroom?) Community means to share, cooperate, compromise, and let others go first. It's far easier to run for my private room, or jump into my private car and drive to my terribly important meeting. It's much easier to escape my longing for intimacy by joining another crowd of people with whom I do not have to be intimate or by turning on a television set.

That's the crux of the matter: Intimacy requires the willingness to live with interpersonal conflict, the commitment to work through differences and problems in order to stay close to one another.

The ideal for the domestic church/family may be the readiness to accept the painful times for the sake of continued closeness and a living family community. There is one aspect of an authentic family spirituality here: I accept the cross of conflict because I know that it is necessary if we are to continue to experience the resurrection joy of family unity. In the long run, it's the only way.

Another positive step some families take is that of scheduling a regular family meeting. This is time set aside not so much for nourishing family relationships directly (though in its own way the family meeting definitely contributes to this). Rather, it is time to "work." We deal with practical issues and resolve conflicts. The family meeting is a time to air difficulties, voice gripes, make decisions, assign household tasks. A family meeting may be the ideal time to decide where we will go for our vacation, or decide what kinds of shared Lenten or Christmas activities we will have this year.

At the family meeing, parents can share with youngsters some of the important decisions that will have an impact on the entire family. What about this new job Dad has been offered that would mean moving half-way across the country? Mom thinks she would like to quit her part-time job and return to school. What do the kids think about her not being there when they come home in the afternoon? The more parents share such issues and decisions with their offspring, the more included, trusted, and valued kids are likely to feel.

All kinds of practical issues are dealt with in a family meeting. One family tells the story of their four-year-old boy who brought up objections to being required to take a daily nap. Another family—a single-parent family—swears that their relationships with one another depend on the regular family meeting. This gives them time that can be counted on when the single-parent family's often unique issues can be faced and dealt with creatively. The single parent in this family—a mother—refers to this regular family meeting as "our life-line to one another."

It is surely appropriate to place the emphasis today on the need for family togetherness times. If the family/domestic church is to be any kind of Christian community at all, there must be regular quality time together. But it is well to remember that each family member is also an individual. Words of the great Trappist monk and hermit, Thomas Merton, come to mind: "Are our efforts to be more 'communal' and to be more 'family' really genuine, or are they only new ways to be intolerant of the solitude and integrity of the individual person?" (Contemplation in a World of Action).

It is important for families to value time for the individual to be alone. But "privacy" is not the theme here. "Privacy" tends to be a little more than a socially acceptable way to talk about avoiding other people. We have already seen that such "privacy" can have destructive effects on a family. Rather, the alone time that is important for the Christian family is best described as "solitude." It is in times of solitude and quiet that the individual can form some of his or her deepest convictions about life and about his or her relationships with other members of the family. It is one of the paradoxes of solitude that when I experience time in this "holy aloneness" that my relationships with others are nourished in special ways. I do not seek solitude as an escape from life or from my family. On the contrary, I enter into solitude in order to renew my relationship with the Holy One who remains at the very heart of my relationships with the other members of my family.

Families that strive to become Christian communities will do all they can to encourage their members to love this kind of solitude. Parents can best model a love for solitude—for time alone with oneself and God—for children of all ages by simply talking about their own need for solitary time and how good it is for them. Then, perhaps of most importance, they can follow through on their words by actually making regular time for solitary thought, meditative reading, and quiet prayer. I cannot give some peace, a bit of wisdom, and a spirit of joy to my family, unless I first gain these for myself.

Some families schedule a day or a weekend every month or two for each parent—and each child who is old enough—to be away at a local retreat house, house of prayer, or some other valued place of solitude. (There is a great need for places such as houses of prayer to be sensitive to the unique scheduling needs of families, especially, who rarely can set aside large blocks of time for retreats and yet need to have time for prayerful solitude—even if there is a thirty-day retreat for priests or sisters going on. It is very frustrating for family people to call a house of prayer and be told that they cannot spend a day there because the place is packed with sisters who are making a thirty-day retreat. Thirty days! This is an unheard of luxury falling on the ears of a parent. Could not one room be kept unoccupied by a house of prayer, even during the heavy summer retreat months, for family people whose spiritual needs continue to exist?)

Family members then talk—as part of a Family Night, around the dinner table or at some other natural time—about their solitary times, about what they have learned or gained. This tends to inspire a healthy curiosity in kids about spending time in solitude, too, as they become older.

There is perhaps no greater gift parents can offer their children than the gift of a love for regular quiet time alone—time to think, to get to know oneself and God. In today's society, where "the crowd" tends to dominate the individual (especially during the teen years), such youngsters may be more likely to grow up with an ability to think for themselves and act as mature Christians, rather than wander through life going along in order to get along.

There is a need for families to be together; a need for children and parents to stay in touch, to talk, to share their lives, their hopes and dreams, their memories, their fears and anxieties. Sacrifices may need to be made on a regular basis in order for such times to happen. But there is a need, also, for individual family members to become strong in themselves, in what they believe and in their relationship with Christ. For this, regular times of prayerful solitude are of vital importance. By being solitary in fruitful ways and by being together in ways that nourish family intimacy, the Christian family can become an authentic Christian community of faith, hope, and love.

It is this life as a Christian family community that forms the basis for all that remains to be said here about a spirituality for Christian families.

Chapter 2

THE FAMILY AS A SERVANT CHURCH

SCRIPTURE scholars tell us that the very core of the message of Jesus may be found in Mark 1:15. There Jesus begins his public ministry with these words: "This is the time of fulfillment. The reign of God is at hand! Reform your lives and believe in the gospel!"

There are two parts ot this message of Jesus. One part communicates comfort; the other is meant to unsettle us and send us forth on the Christian trek. First, Jesus says that "the reign of God is at hand." These are words of comfort, words that tell us of the eruption of God's love in human history in a unique manner, as well as in our personal lives. Now there is no need for fear or anxiety, because just behind life and the universe, indeed bursting into our ordinary days when it is least expected, is the boundless love of God.

But then the other shoe falls. Jesus says, "Reform your lives and believe in the gospel." The gospel, of course, is the reality of God's love for us, and we are invited to turn away from self-centered pursuits, from dependence on false gods, in order to believe in and depend on that love alone. This is the only way God can be known for real. We are called to empty our hearts of fear and distrust, to turn loose of false gods with their false promises and embrace the true God alone, and one another in authentic caring love.

In other words, the church—and in a special way, the church that is the family—is invited by Christ to live a life centered on God and neighbor above all else. The neighbor we are called to love first, of course, is the other members of my family. But it can't stop there. There is a real danger that a family may turn in on itself. We may begin to feel so cozy and warm in our family relationships that we forget the call to reach out to others. Just as the church at large is sent to minister to those outside the community who have special needs, so the family-church is sent by Christ to touch the lives of those in the wider community with the love and peace with which they themselves have been gifted by the Spirit.

To reach out to those who do not belong to our immediate family is an essential part of a family spirituality. There is no better illustration of just how important this is than the story of the sheep and the goats told by Jesus in Matthew 25. This is the only place in the New Testament where the believing community is told explicitly what will determine one's eternal destiny. Notice that the message is not that one must believe certain doctrines or go to church on Sunday. These things become important, of course, but only in a secondary or derivative way. The critical question has to do with meeting the needs of those who thirst, who hunger, those who are in need of clothing and those in jail. What matters in the end is meeting basic human needs with compassionate action. This is the mark of a faith that is more than words and pious genuflections.

The family/domestic church is invited by the Christ who dwells in the family's midst to regularly turn outward to others, to overcome the temptation to turn in on itself. So the Christian family will naturally feel impelled to discover the way or ways in which they can best put their gifts at the service of others. Whatever decision is made about this, one basic principle is

especially important to keep in mind. Whatever the
family decides to do to serve others, it is imperative
that it be some form of service that the whole family
can become involved in *together*. Serving others ought
not to become just another way of fragmenting the
family! This would be self-defeating.

In *David Copperfield*, Charles Dickens paints a
brilliant literary portrait of the classic do-gooder,
whose many works of "charity" constantly cause her
own family to suffer. Mrs. Jellyby is forever dashing
away to save poor people on the other side of the world,
while at home her own children are dirty and ill cared
for, and her husband is sullen and withdrawn. This is
an extreme example, of course, but Mrs. Jellyby's situation illustrates the kind of thing that could happen if
parents, say, become so involved in "helping others"
that they spend less and less time with their own
children. This may be an excellent way to incur resentment in the hearts of the children which could easily be
transferred, perhaps unconsciously, to Christianity and
the church as a whole.

Instead, when the family regularly serves together
this has positive impact on both parents and children.
Indeed, involvement in out-reach activities alongside
their parents is one of the best forms of "religious
education" any youngster can receive. This way
children learn from experience that faith is a way of
life, that a Christian commitment makes a real difference in the ways one chooses to use the time of one's
life.

Service activities generously pursued make it almost
impossible for a charge of hypocrisy to be leveled at
parents—a charge teenage offspring have on more than

one occasion been know to level against parents who
appear to be little more than "Sunday Christians."

No suggestion is made, of course, that the Christian
family is required to become a miniature St. Vincent De
Paul Society. Rare families do choose to orient their entire life toward serving others—for example, by becoming as a family members of a Catholic Worker House of
Hospitality. Now and then whole families will join
Maryknoll or another overseas missionary society for a
few years. But for most families the need to serve
others is integrated into ordinary day-to-day life.

The ways families choose to do this are as varied as
families themselves. But perhaps the most basic spirit
that characterizes this aspect of a family spirituality is
one of hospitality—a spirited openness to others from
outside the family circle. This spirit of hospitality finds
its roots in the practice of the earliest Christian families
who set aside a "Christ room" in their homes for the
wandering pilgrim. This is a tradition which has largely been lost sight of. Even so, many modern families
would find it a luxury indeed to be able to let a whole
bedroom sit empty most of the time.

But the authentic spirit of hospitality is another matter. This is a spirit that receives the visitor or guest with
open arms. Parents set the tone for the family in this
regard. Any parish seems to have its more obvious examples, the families who are forever inviting others
over to dinner on Sunday afternoons. Many a parish has
its unofficial "welcome family," the family which has
an abundance of warmth, humor, and cheerful conversation but is not interested in impressing anyone with
their house, which is usually filled with furniture that
stopped trying to look new long ago and kitchen walls

covered with the scrawled drawings of children. Invited to the home of such a family, the guest can count
on not being treated like a guest. Instead, you find
yourself helping to put together the lasagna or toss the
salad. Or you may be put to work setting the table, after
having been "forced" to take a beer or glass of wine.

Every shape of chair in the house may be drummed
into service as family and guests gather around the
table. Table prayer is likely to be more boistrous than
reverent, and gasps of mock horror are likely to greet
the guests' offer to help clear the table and wash the
dishes.

Some families seem to have a special gift for taking in
foster or adoptive children. Such families often have
many stories to tell of how their life and the lives of
their long-term guests have been changed and enriched
by this form of ministry. Very often the parents' own
"birth children" consider themselves to be as involved
and important to the success of these efforts as are the
adults. This form of service is special indeed, in that it
brings the most intimate fabric of the family's life to
bear on the lives of youngsters who often have known
precious little love in their few years.

Another form of service that is becoming more common is that of providing a temporary home for girls or
young women who are pregnant and unmarried, during the time when they are awaiting the birth of their
babies. In a time when so much is heard about the abor-
tion issue, this is a concrete way in which those who
claim to be "pro-life" can put flesh on their words. It is
relatively easy to point the finger of accusation at those
who undergo abortions. It is quite another thing to offer an alternative which will take the form of time,

money, concern, and the need for a whole family to adapt lovingly to the presence of a new member—and one struggling with a "crisis situation," at that—for several months.

In recent years it has become not unusual at all for groups of married couples to band together to help engaged couples prepare for marriage. One group of couples decided that they wanted to be involved in such a program, but they did not want to leave their children to the care of others in order to do this. So they worked together to design a program independent of any national-level organization, which allows them to bring their children along. Indeed, it was designed so the children would not only just "be there," but would contribute in a positive way to the quality of the experience offered to the engaged couples.

The program is organized in a weekend format and held at a retreat center, as many are. But children are expected to be there and to be in evidence. During registration times, recreation, and meals, the engaged couples naturally interact with the children. During times when the married couples are working with the engaged couples in formal ways, the teenagers and older children care for the younger ones. Thus the overall atmosphere established is one not just of marriage, but of family. It is typical for engaged couples who attend this program to comment positively on the contribution made to their learning experience by the children. They remark on how much more realistic it is to attend a marriage preparation program with children around than to have a more "sterile," adults-only experience—as if children would not someday be an important part of marriage for them, too.

In another part of the country, families for miles
around participate in a hot meal program sponsored by
an inner-city parish. Teams have been organized so
that a different team prepares, brings in, and serves a
hot meal each evening of the month, six nights a week.
On most teams there are families with children of all
ages. It is moving for the newcomer to witness moms,
dads, and kids all serving up the simple but nutritious
food on a bitterly cold winter evening to the street people, the winos, the bums, the poor, and the kicked-
around. Together, families then sit down to share the
food. Everyone gives, everyone receives. Little chidren
chat and giggle with grizzled, dirty men who a few
minutes before were swearing and cursing the fates out
on a street corner. Housewives and "working mothers"
tell bag ladies about the recipe for that evening's hash
or dessert. Even the emotionally or mentally disturbed
"guests" who choose to keep to themselves in some corner of the hall seem to benefit from the spirit brought to
this gathering by families.

On the meal ticket each person receives before enter-
ing to eat are these words: "Welcome to the Lord's Ban-
quet, the Miracle of Loaves and Fishes." Although the
distinctions blur considerably between those who are
"doing" and those who are being "done unto," this is
another way in which families, as families, reach out to
others. Thus, not only do they help those who have less,
but they keep before their mind's eye the easily forgotten truth that the world is bigger than just their family
with its small agonies and ecstasies.

One family happened to inherit a small lake cabin,
not a terribly fancy one, but one that "serves." Since
they can usually inhabit the cabin only on weekends,

they invite friends and relatives, the parish priest, and the people next door to use it whenever they are free to do so. This family believes they have been given their cabin not just for themselves alone, but to share with others, too.

Another family spent several summer weekends helping an elderly neighbor fix up her house, which had sadly deteriorated since her husband's death. They did yard work, painted, cleaned and repaired screens, storm windows, and plumbing. This family is typical of families who are simply sensitive to the needs of others as they arise and not so tied up by their own plans and schedules that they cannot respond spontaneously and without fanfare to the ordinary needs of a neighbor.

A young couple with no children of their own yet hops in their car to spend most of one Saturday a month driving around to the homes of others collecting reusable baby supplies for redistribution by a pregnancy-care agency in their town. Thus they resist the unique kind of narcissism which can so easily afflict the lives of young childless couples in our society today.

One of the activities Jesus mentions in the Matthew 25 story of the sheep and goats is visiting those in prison. What would the impact be if families from parishes located near prisons were to develop ways to serve prisoners and their families? A very simple way for a family to touch the life of a prisoner is to correspond with him or her by mail. Such a commitment may lead to a personal visit at the prison later on, but whether this happens or not both the life of the prisoner and the life of the family will be affected in ways consistent with the gospel.

There are as many ways for families to serve others as there are families. The crucial thing is for family members to know that they are called by Christ to engage in what used to be known as "the corporal works of mercy." The family is called to give of its time and resources regularly in order to care for those who have special needs, be they physical, emotional, or material. This is where the faith that is ritualized in family prayer and in the parish takes on a credibility that can be recognized a mile away.

Chapter 3

THE FAMILY PRAYS AND CELEBRATES

ORDINARILY, when "family spirituality" is mentioned the first thing people think of is family prayer and other explicit forms of family piety. It should be clear by now that family prayer is but one part of a total family spirituality. Too, it must be said from the outset that family prayer and celebration are *expressions* or manifestations of the family's identity as a Christian community. They are not the thing itself. What makes the family Christian is a common dedication to Christ and the shared ongoing attempt to live the spirit of the gospel. The family is not Christian, is not the foundational church, first of all because the family prays together. Rather, it is because of the faith of the family, the shared personal relationship with the risen Christ, that the family prays and celebrates its faith in various ways. Prayer and celebration are expressions before they are causes of faith. Prayer and family liturgies strengthen and nourish our faith as a family. But they are meaningful only to the extent that they are expressions of a family faith that is already there.

Granted, this sounds like something of a chicken-and-egg business, asking which comes first, faith or prayer. But the purpose of going into the issue is to establish the fact that a family does not become Christian or religious merely by praying, but by dedicating itself to Christ and to love of God and neighbor. Only then does family prayer and liturgy attain its most complete character as a way of both nourishing and fulfilling the identity of the family as a Christian community.

That said, it is true that an indispensable part of a family sprituality is regular shared prayer and family rituals. The most important principle is this: Family prayer and family ritual ought never to be imposed or artificial. It is more accurate to say that family prayer must be allowed to emerge from within the fabric of family life itself. We can't make it happen so much as we can nourish its growth in our midst.

The life of the family is itself holy. It is a mistake to act as if we must make it holy by artificial means. The family is a faith community—or is called to be such. All that need be done is to look at the life of the family and to discover the naturally sacred events that already take place there. The family recognizes the sacred character of these events and takes simple steps to celebrate that sacred character through prayer and ritual.

It is absolutely critical to begin with the most obvious aspects of family life. Start small and keep it simple. For example, there is no more holy event in the life of a family than the family meal. The family's evening meal is naturally eucharistic. At the evening meal much more can be shared than food. There are opportunities for some prayer, a bit of song, a lighted candle, a brief holding of hands around the table. It is by taking some simple steps that the family meal can be rescued from its current position on the "endangered species" list.

Granted, dinnertime can be filled with noise and conflict, sometimes degenerating into near chaos. People jump up from the table at odd times. The baby is screaming, there are arguments over who got the biggest piece of cake and what so-and-so *really* said at school that day. All the same, the family's evening meal has the potential to be much more. It can be an explicitly sacred event, too, at least some of the time.

It helps if you can start when children are little. Build traditions around the family table. When our three children were hardly even talking we began the tradition of singing the refrain from, "O Come, O Come, Emmanuel" as the beginning of our grace before dinner during the Advent season. It wasn't long before the little ones were joining in. Even the crying baby would clam up and gaze in delighted wonder around the table at his singing family. Oh, it took Dad and Mom a few evenings of this before a bit of embarrassment at singing in that situation wore off. But just try to call off the singing once and see what a storm of protest would be raised from the hearts of children. It wasn't long before we were singing during the Christmas and Easter seasons, too. And now we are to the point where we sing the refrain from one song or another virtually every evening of the year.

Evening mealtime needs to be "off limits" for the Christian family. "Is nothing sacred anymore?" goes the saying. For the Christian family the evening meal must be kept sacred. This does not mean that there should not be an exception now and then. But as a general rule, all should be present, even when sacrifices must be made for this to be so. This is the one time of day when we promise to be there for one another. The running will stop, the world will turn loose of us as individuals, and we *will* be a family for an hour or so. In the long run, nothing that takes us away from one another is as important as our relationships within the family. Nothing. Therefore, we join hands for prayer around a lighted candle—even if Tommy is only holding Linda's little finger because tonight girls are "yucky." We are family because of the real presence of Christ in our midst—where two or three (or four or five or six. . .) are gathered together in his name.

The family meal is the time for celebrating in simple but meaningful ways special days, both sacred and secular. For, since the Son of God has shared our life and our world as one of us, really all times and all events are holy; the secular is inseparable from the sacred. Even events in our lives that appear to have no sacred dimension do include the sacred if we will but look a little closer.

One of the most obvious secular-sacred events is a birthday. When a family gathers to celebrate the birthday of one of its members around the dinner table, more is marked than the passage of the anniversary of a birth. What is birth? It is creation, the coming into existence of the totally new and unique. To celebrate a birthday is to pause to wonder anew at the gift of this person to the rest of us. We thank God for Sean, our first-born. We celebrate Gretchen or Erin or Joseph, Mom or Dad. We light the candles on the cake—in addition to the usual Christ candle on the table—and sing "Happy Birthday." But we also say a special prayer of thanks for the birthday person, mentioning his or her special qualities or special events in the life of this person since last year's birthday. We pray to acknowledge that birthday gifts remind us of the birthday person who is the most valued gift of all today.

For some time now we have kept a "Family Book of Days," a three-ring binder filled with blank pages, pages being filled now with reminders of significant dates in the life of our family, in the lives of our extended family and friends, and in the lives of saints and

other remarkable people we admire. There is one page
for each day of the year. Open the book to today's date:
There is the reminder that today is the feast of St. Clare.
Did you know she is the patron saint of television? Turn
another page: Next week will mark the anniversary of
the death of Thomas Merton. Last month we remembered the anniversary of the birth of Dorothy Day, and
before long we will be reminded of the day on which
our second son took his first steps. Remember the day
Patrick fell out of the apple tree and broke his arm?
How about the time Aunt Barbara gave birth to twins!
Here is the day the Wright Brothers made their first
flight at Kitty Hawk—which is also Dad's birthday!

Part of the evening meal ritual is to open and read
the Family Book of Days, just before prayer (when
everyone is more or less quieted down). This is one way
we build family traditions.

In this way we help preserve our shared memories
which give us strength and much joy. It is, in great part,
our shared memories that bond us to one another, that
make us in truth a family. In this way, too, we remember that we are part of a much larger family, one that
transcends both history and geographical location. Our
larger family—traditionally called "the communion of
saints"—spans the centuries and encompasses both
heaven and earth. With all of these we are one, we are
family.

Many typical events—both special and ordinary—can
be appropriately observed with prayer and simple
rituals around the family table. This is important,
because in this way a normal, natural event is given a
special meaning; the family is not asked to gather on
some artificial pretext, and the family's ordinary life is

not disrupted by prayer and ritual. Instead, the ordinary family meal is allowed to express the sacred
dimensions of the family's life that are always there.

Some of the most unlikely "secular" events lend
themselves to sacred celebrations around the family
dinner table. Say a teenager receives his or her driver's
license. Light the Christ candle on the table in the usual
manner. Include in the table prayer a petition for the
safety of the young driver (and of the family car!) but include also an acknowledgement of the new level of
responsibility and maturity this event signals in the life
of the young person. Include a prayer of thanks for the
driver's test successfully passed. Pray that the faith of
the young person may grow along with this sign of
secular maturity. Conclude with a round of applause
from the entire family.

How about the first day of school? Or the beginning
of a new job or career? The anticipated beginning of a
family journey the next morning lends itself beautifully
to the use of some of the traditional prayers for going
on a journey. The list of events that can be celebrated
around the family table goes on and on. Only a bit of
creativity and courage are required.

There are other natural events in the life of the family
that lend themselves to ritual and prayer. Going to sleep
and waking up are laden with religious meaning. As
the pastors of the domestic church, parents have the
privilege of blessing their children. From their
youngest years, children may be given parental bless-
ings at bedtime. The parent simply traces the sign of
the cross on the child's forehead—as he or she did at
the child's baptism—and says, "God bless you,"
"Christ's peace be with you," or some other simple

prayer. Then conclude by placing your hand on the child's head. Or think up some way of doing this that you are most comfortable with. Children love this blessing and soon would not think of going to bed without it.

Finally, there are the more obvious liturgical seasons of the year which lend themselves to family home celebrations. Advent is time for the Advent calendar. It's surprising how affection for this calendar maintains a hold on children, even when they become "too old" for such things. This is the season, of course, for a family Advent wreath, to be lighted every evening for the family meal in place of the usual single Christ candle.

Then comes Christmastime. Make of the decorating of the home and of the tree a time when the often missed sacred nature of Christmas is remembered. Put some sacred Christmas music on the record player or stereo. Have a blessing of the tree and of the manger scene as well.

During Lent substitute a dish of sand or an old dead branch from a tree (small, of course) for the Christ candle on the table. Begin the family grace with the refrain from a favorite Lenten song. Revive an old parish custom and adapt it for the home: Cover all religious art in the home with a purple cloth—the crucifix, an icon on the wall, or a statue. This can have profound impact on children, as a very tangible way of marking the season.

Next, of course, comes Easter. Use an Easter song for the table prayer. Bring back the Christ candle. Bake an Easter bread. Decorate eggs and talk about the egg as a symbol for the Resurrection. Especially when children are old enough, be sure the family goes together to the

midnight Easter liturgy. Rising in the darkness of the
early spring adds to the drama of the liturgy with its
symbols of fire and water, of darkness, light, and ex-
ultation. Go to almost any lengths to avoid a dull,
lifeless liturgy on Easter! For in such there is probably
some kind of "sin."

There are so many good resource books on family
prayer and celebration that this chapter is being kept
purposely brief and sketchy. Yet, finally, this must be
said: Family prayer and family home liturgies are
learned slowly. They cannot, in truth, be taught. Any
"recipe" that is offered must be adapted and modified
by the individual family. Each family must learn by
trial and error and success what is good for this family
and what is not.

There are problems to be overcome, too. There is the
pain of the family where one parent is interested but
the other is reluctant. Teens, unless they grew up with
family prayer—and sometimes even then—sometimes
resist any suggestion that they participate in a family
ritual. These are difficult situations, and there are no
magic solutions.

In the end, a family prays by praying. You begin by
beginning. The question, "How can we pray as a family?" is answered only with encouragement to begin, to
be patient with yourselves and with one another, and to
be persistent. The family that starts in little ways, that
does not expect to become a family that prays with ease
at the drop of a saint's feast day, is most likely to suc-
ceed, by degrees.

The secret of all prayer, including family prayer, is to
begin by quietly praying for the gift of prayer. In pray-

ing together around your table for the gift of prayer, you begin to pray. Your prayer will have already been answered, and prayer will bloom in your midst, growing and nourishing the spirit of family life—not without purposeful efforts and not without some sacrifice, but nourishing the life of the family in hidden ways all the same.

Chapter 4

MARRIAGE: FOUNDATION FOR THE DOMESTIC CHURCH

THE very bottom line in the traditional nuclear family is the relationship of wife and husband. Upon the relationship of the couple depends the quality of life in the family as a whole. As Jesuit theologian Karl Rahner has made clear, the married couple constitutes the smallest authentic form of church: "In marriage the church is made present. It is really the smallest community, the smallest, but at the same time the true community of the redeemed and the sanctified . . . the smallest, but at the same time the genuine individual church."

Therefore, the sacrament of marriage is best understood as a specific way of being church, of living as a Christian community. It is the vocation of the married couple to go about being Christian precisely by being married to one another.

Let's be even more precise about this. The most basic of all the sacraments is baptism. It is through baptism that the Christian life begins, that life in Christ is inaugurated. The sacraments of vocation—holy orders and matrimony—are ways of living out one's baptismal commitment, ways of channeling one's Christian life along specific lines. A spirituality of marriage, then, can best be understood in those ways in which the couple lives out the baptismal commitment in their relationship with one another, first of all, and then in their relationships with their children and with the rest of the world. But it must always be kept in mind that uppermost in the spirituality of marriage is the intimacy of husband and wife.

In order to understand a spirituality of marriage it becomes, therefore, crucial to have a prior understanding of baptism. For only if baptism is correctly understood can marriage be accurately viewed as a way of living out the baptismal promises.

In years past, baptisms were as a rule held off in a corner of the parish church in a very private manner, when nothing else of importance was going on and the church was otherwise virtually empty. So about the only time Catholics witnessed a baptism was when their own children were born, or when they were asked to be godparents to someone else's child. And even then the baptismal ceremony was wrapped in Latin, so a complete understanding of the sacrament was hardly communicated by the baptismal liturgy itself.

Today, however, it is more common for infant and adult baptisms to be celebrated in the context of regularly scheduled parish Masses—and, of course, in the vernacular. So the entire congregation is reminded several times a year of the promises that are made at baptism and of the beliefs that are affirmed. The words of the baptismal liturgy are more familiar today than they have been for centuries. But what overall meaning is intended by those words?

Perhaps baptism can be understood today by calling on concepts from the Fourth Gospel. There the Christian community learns that as disciples of Christ they live *in* the world and *for* the world but that the Christian is not to be *of* the world. In other words, Christians are to be closely involved in the concerns of the world but according to a different set of values and standards than those which are embraced by the world insofar as it is unaffected by the Spirit of Christ. This also means that the Christian recognizes and celebrates and takes

joy in the world since it is created by God and redeemed by Christ. The Christian rejects the world only
insofar as it is less than it is intended by God to be.

According to the gospel tradition, therefore, the
Christian's priorities are different. For the Christian,
the meaning of life is found in relationships with God
and neighbor. This is why Jesus teaches that the
greatest commandment is to love God with one's whole
being and one's neighbor as oneself. This is radical talk!
For the Christian's life is to be focused entirely on a
dedication to love of God and neighbor. This idea is so
central to the Christian perspective that in the only
place in any of the gospels (Matthew 25) that Jesus
discusses what will determine one's eternal destiny he
zeros right in on the need to care for one's neighbor.
Jesus identifies the love of God with compassionate action on behalf of those with special human needs. He
says that if you visited those in prison, clothed the nak-
ed, or fed the hungry, then, in fact, you did it for him.

The heart of the Christian life is compassionate love
of God and neighbor, and the two cannot be separated.
The business of going to church on Sunday and of
believing certain doctrines all adds up to something
that is secondary—important, but secondary all the
same. When people remarked on the lives of the first
Christians, they did not say, "Those Christians, see
how they go to church and believe certain doctrines!"
Sounds ludicrous, doesn't it? No, as everyone knows,
the comment was, "See those Christians, how they love
one another!" This is what makes the Christian different; this is what being a follower of Christ is most
basically all about: a dedication to loving action on
behalf of God and other people as the most fundamen-

tal standard upon which one's daily life is based. It's as simple, as radical—and as difficult—as that.

If marriage is to be correctly understood, then, and if a Christian spirituality of marriage is to be made explicit, it must be done in light of precisely this understanding of the Christian life. The Christian life is a matter of living very much in the world and on behalf of the world and its concerns but according to a set of values and attitudes which place love of God and neighbor at the very heart of one's life. So this is what Christian marriage is about: going about the business of living in and for the world—of loving the world—by placing love of God and other people uppermost.

But this understanding needs to be made still more precise. The point here is that spouses are the smallest form of church because they dedicate themselves to love of God and neighbor as married people. Every expression they may give to their faith is conditioned by this fact. In every sense, the married partners go about being followers of Christ in the world most basically by being married to one another. To paraphrase St. Paul, they may give all they have to feed the poor and hand over their bodies to be burned, but if they do not have a living and lively marriage it profits them nothing.

So this gets to the heart of the matter. For Christian spouses, the "neighbor" that is to be loved is first of all the person to whom one is married. To nourish and give regular attention to the marriage relationship is central to the couple's living of the Christian life. The couple's religious life is not something apart from their daily life together; rather, it remains at the very heart of their marital experience.

To paraphrase from the New Testament again (1

John): If anyone says, "My love is fixed on God," but fails to love his or her spouse, that person is a liar. One who shows no love for the spouse he or she can see every morning across the breakfast table cannot love the God he or she has not seen. The commandment we have from God is this: Whoever loves God must also love his or her spouse in ways that can be felt.

This may sound a bit dreamy and idealistic, like a lot of nice words that almost anyone would agree with—and then promptly forget. Perhaps the question to ask at this point is: So what?

We have here a set of ideas which, if correctly understood, lead to a perspective on life that runs directly counter to a view of marriage that dominates the lives of many married couples. The contention is that for the Christian married couple there is nothing more important than the ongoing love and intimacy shared by wife and husband. A contrary perspective tends to hold the upper hand today. The prevailing belief is that a happy marriage depends upon all kinds of material and economic realities, realities which end up taking first place in the life of the couple. This is an attitude toward marriage that is encouraged by a consumer culture, even from the moment the engagement is first announced. The message broadcast in many ways to engaged couples is that the future success of their marriage depends on how much money they spend on the engagement ring. Then their future happiness depends on how elaborate the wedding and reception can be. Next, the more money the couple spends on their honeymoon, the more likely that their marriage will be a good one. And we're off and running: Your marriage will be all it can be if only you have a big beautiful house filled with new furniture and appliances (even if you find it necessary to go into great debt for this to be possible); and of course you really do need a brand new car before you will feel really married.

This may sound ridiculous. But it is important to realize that, even if a married couple would not agree with such messages as stated here, everyone is affected by the commercialization of marriage. Such messages about marriage are presented in hundreds of ways daily by a mass media advertising industry that is almost inescapable. Those who manufacture products and offer services to consumers don't pay millions of dollars a year for those 30-and sixty-second ads on television because they like to spend the money—they do it because it *works*; and the same can be said for all forms of advertising. They work. Everyone is affected by mass media advertising, even though in many cases they are unaware of it. The advertising industry does a very effective job of forming personal values of a highly materialistic nature.

Of course, once the couple is married the same set of materialistic and commerical values begin to take other forms. You won't be truly good parents unless you buy all kinds of special furniture, clothes, and gadgets—not to mention toys—for your baby. Your effectiveness as parents is determined by the *things* you buy for your child: That's the message.

But it takes money to buy everything from the engagement ring to the house and car and baby paraphernalia. So what becomes number one in the life of the married couple? You guessed it: jobs and careers as means to the accumulation of money and posses-

sions. Husband and wife may continue to say that their
marriage is most important for them, but their actions
reveal their belief that marital happiness depends on
things outside their relationship: jobs, money, and the
accumulation of more and more material possessions.
The marital relationship is neglected in the pursuit of
greater affluence.

A priest we know once told us of a young man who
came to him with this account of his situation: "Father,
Jane and I are getting a divorce. I just *can't* understand
it. She has a job that brings in $20,000 a year. I make
about $30,000. We have a big beautiful house, two cars,
and a lake cabin. Last summer we took a vacation in
Hawaii. Why is our marriage ending in divorce?"

Any married couple needs a certain minimum income, a decent place to live, and enough food to eat and
clothes to wear. And all of these require the regular ap-
pearance of pay checks. Unemployment or the lack of
an adequate income can have terribly destructive effects on a marriage. But the point is that as Americans
we tend to always want more, to never be satisfied with
what we have. We tend to believe in our secret heart of
hearts that the accumulation of ever more money and
attaining of a yet higher degree of affluence will lead to
personal happiness. We really do tend to think that our
marriage will be better once we have more money or a
bigger house or a new car. We really do believe family
relationships will improve once we don't have to watch
our pennies so closely. The mistake is in acting as if the
quality of our marriage depends on things outside the
marital relationship itself. To repeat, certain mini-
mums are necessary: clothes, food, a roof over our
heads. But how much is really needed to be happy?

Very little, really, by typical American standards. Most of us have more than enough, if we stop to think about it. It's time to shift attention to our marriage, to the continuing impact spouses have on one another. It is time to spend regular time on us, even (perhaps especially) if it means spending less time on the job or career.

Another tactic married couples frequently find convenient for avoiding one another is the children. We want to provide the children with all the things we never had. Or we feel guilty if we are away from the children when we could be with them. It is, of course, important for parents and children to have plenty of regular time together. But what kids need most is parents who have a healthy, happy marriage. There is a limit to the amount of time parents can spend with their children before they reach a point of diminishing returns, as it were.

One of the best things parents can do for their children—no matter what the ages of the kids—is to get away from them at least twice a month and simply enjoy being a married couple. It is important to spend time and some money on your marriage. Sacrifices will have to be made. Personally, we have spent more than a little money on evenings out and sitters. This is money that could have been saved or spent on nice new "things." Instead, we spend it on us, on dinners out, on movies we attend together, on plays we want to see or concerts we enjoy together.

Of course, money is not the point. A regular evening out together can be as simple as cups of coffee or hot chocolate shared together in a quiet cafe. The point is the time together away from the kids. The kids will thank you for it. And when the kids are gone—which they will be far sooner than you think—you will still know one another, instead of being virtual strangers.

The underlying conviction is that marriage is not a static relationship between two static people. Marriage is a process or set of processes to which a man and woman commit themselves. Marriage is a woman and a man who promise to be there for one another. And so they must *be there*, not just physically in the same room for breakfast and dinner with the kids, but emotionally, psychologically, and spiritually, on a regular basis. They must be there with one another in an undivided way, to talk, to listen, to have some simple fun together once a week or so. After all, isn't this why people get married in the first place?

Don't be fooled. It takes time and discipline to be sure that you have quality time together regularly. It means getting out the calendar and putting *yourselves* on it right along with the PTA meetings and the hours of volunteer work.

What it all comes down to is taking the trouble to be sure that the other person *feels* loved and not taken for granted. It has been said that the opposite of love is not hate, but indifference. It feels terrible to think that you are taken for granted. Fragile beings that we are, we need to be reminded in ways we can feel that we are special, loved, valued, and cared for.

This is a great part of what married love is meant to be for Christian believers: the experience of God's love through the love of my spouse. I can't really know God's love unless my spouse loves me in ways that help me to feel loved. My spouse can tell me about it (and words of love are important) but words alone tend to lose their power. I need to be shown. Bring me flowers;

fix my favorite dinner even though it takes more work than you like; take the kids to the park so I can have a quiet afternoon around the house; spend some money we can't afford to spend for some small gift you know will really speak your love for me.

To nourish marital intimacy is what a spirituality of marriage is all about. Sometimes this means that I must struggle to overcome residual aspects of myself from my past that keep us from being closer. Perhaps my mother passed along to me feelings about my sexuality that make it difficult for me to experience the fullness of joy and pleasure in our sexual love-making. Maybe as a woman I don't feel as attractive to you as you say I am. As a man, perhaps I have a difficult time being anything but the aggressor when we make love. Or maybe I find it tough to be really tender or to tell you about my fears and anxieties. I think I could overcome these negative residuals in myself that hinder our relationship, but I need your help—and I do not find it easy to ask for your help with something so personal, such a sensitive part of myself.

There is perhaps no more powerful way in which a married couple experiences the spiritual quality of their relationship than when they make love. It has been suggested that sexual love-making and intercourse are for the Christian couple an actual celebration of the sacrament of marriage. Spirit cannot be separated from body; bodily love cannot be separated from spiritual love. So it is part of the ascesis or discipline of a marital spirituality to love one another in every dimension of our relationship, to celebrate with joy, passion, pleasure, and peace our love through sexual love-making, and to strive to overcome anything

which handicaps the full celebration and renewal of
our relationship through sexual ecstasy.

Still another aspect of the discipline of a marital
spirituality—an aspect which demands effort and per-
sistence—is the need to learn effective intimacy skills.
Here, of course, the topic is the broad-based intimacy
which is meant to pervade every aspect of the couple's
relationship. Every couple can use some renewal of
their communication skills. It is a fact of modern life
that no marriage can hope to weather the predictable
and unpredictable events of a shared life without know-
ing how to communicate effectively. Couples must go
to the trouble to learn the practical skills that are
available to them which can facilitate communication
rather than allow it to be a kind of hit-or-miss proposi-
tion.

Ideally, youngsters from their earliest days of formal
education would be taught good communication skills.
But be that as it may, couples who are married and who
are getting married today have hardly ever learned the
practical communication skills that are so important to
the quality of their relationship. It is a part of a marital
spirituality to learn these skills and to use them well.

Think back to when you were first going together.
What was it about each other that you found most in-
triguing? What was it you found to spend so much time
talking about? It was, of course, your individu-
ality—your different interests, your unique perspectives on life, your delightfully special way of being you.
It is highly beneficial to a marriage to keep this in-
dividuality alive, because it contributes to the growth of
your relationship as a couple. There is no room for an
attitude which would view one spouse as somehow incomplete without the other. A marriage is made by two

complete individuals who are perfectly capable of being self-sufficient. Only then is the gift of self to the other possible, for only then do I have a complete self to give.

So it is very nourishing to a marriage for spouses to give one another the time to pursue individual interests and enthusiasms. Each couple will have a balance of together and individual time that fits the unique character of their marriage. But both need to be there. By continuing to be alive and to grow as an individual I can continue to keep myself interesting for my spouse. For one thing, this will continue to provide us with new topics for discussion. This is also a practical way of keeping in mind the fact that I can never know completely the constantly changing, fascinating mystery that is my spouse. Instead, the adventure of discovering one another goes on for a lifetime.

The Christian married couple also shares a life of prayer. Some couples believe that even sexual intimacy is not as personal as one's prayer life. And so for a couple to share prayer in some fashion is to share a dimension of their relationship where the mystery of being called together by God becomes almost tangible. Words become inadequate, perhaps. Maybe the best form of shared prayer for the Christian couple is shared by silent prayer. When husband and wife sit or stand or kneel together and each speaks silently to God the deepest thoughts of his or her heart, at that moment the intimacy of the couple becomes impossible to describe. When wife and husband share spontaneous spoken prayers, there is always at least the slight possibility of feeling the need to "perform" for one's spouse or to meet unspoken expectations.

Regardless of how a couple prays together, however,

to make times for praying together is to allow for space
in the marriage for the Spirit to speak out of the needs
and joys of the marriage to the Father who nourishes
the relationship of the couple in hidden ways.

Finally, there is a need to speak at least briefly about
roles in a Christian marriage. This is a topic that has
many significant implications for the ways in which a
Christian marriage is lived from day to day.

A traditional understanding of marriage has seen the
relationship between husband and wife to be one that is
basically authoritarian. In this view, the husband is
"head" of his wife. He makes all the important decisions, although he may likely consult with his wife. The
wife, for her part, bows to the authority of the husband
in matters of any importance to the marriage and the
family. For social and cultural reasons, this has since
the Industrial Revolution also meant that the husband
was the "breadwinner" and the wife the "homemaker"
and primary nurturer of children.

This traditional understanding of roles in marriage
has roots in a fundamentalist interpretation of the Bible
which led to a "headship" and "submission" model of
marriage. Drawing upon certain Old and New Testament texts, fundamentalist preachers and teachers
have maintained that in the scheme of things provided
for by God in the Bible, the husband was to exercise
"headship" in relation to his wife. The wife, in turn,
was to be submissive to the "headship" of her husband
as her way of relating to Christ. By being submissive to
her husband, the wife exercised submission to the will
of God in her life.

Fundamentalist Christians have traditionally ad-
hered to this interpretation of the Bible. Today a few

Catholic biblical fundamentalists choose to do the same. In essence, they teach that a couple cannot have a truly Christian marriage unless they practice the headship/submission model of marriage provided for by a fundamentalist interpretation of Scripture.

The only support for this opinion is the fundamentalists's own interpretation of the Bible (plus, in a few instances, attempts on the part of Catholic fundamentalists to dredge up what they perceive to be data in support of their position from the social sciences). Nothing in the official teachings of the Catholic Church states that a couple must practice headship and submission. Catholic Scripture scholars overwhelmingly reject the notion that the headship/submission model is the only one acceptable for Christian couples. Numerous statements by John Paul II would, if anything, lend support to a marriage based on the fundamental equality of husband and wife:

> When St. Paul wrote that "wives should be submissive to their husbands as to the Lord," he did not mean that the husband is "boss" of the wife and the interpersonal pact of matrimony is a pact of dominion of husband over wife. There is to be no one-sided domination. Each is to be subject to the other from a sense of Christian piety.

Our own conviction is that it is possible to have a Christian marriage and base that marriage on any number of models insofar as role differentiation is concerned. To one degree or another, most couples marrying today seem to prefer a model which presumes the basic equality of wife and husband. There is rarely any strong sense of the husband being endowed with a

superior form of authority. This has been called a two-
vote rather than a one-vote marriage. When important
decisions must be made, husband and wife collaborate.

This "companionate" marriage frees husband and
wife to relate to God through one another equally. The
husband is submissive about as often as is the wife. The
practical details of generating income, cleaning the
house, doing the laundry, caring for children, and
preparation of meals are worked out in ways with
which both are comfortable. But the basic equality of
spouses is taken for granted. All practical arrangements in the daily living of marriage and family
life are understood to be open to renegotiation at appropriate times.

Each marriage is unique because it is lived by two
unique invividuals. Every married couple has the right to
develop an understanding of roles in marriage that
works best for that particular couple. Wives and
husbands are perfectly free to agree to a headship/sub-
mission style of marriage if they wish. Other couples
should feel no constraint to do likewise if they prefer a
"companionate" style of being married Chrisitans.

We began this chapter by pointing out that the married couple constitutes the smallest form of church—a
form of church which is nevertheless authentic and
complete. By nourishing the ongoing intimacy of their
relationship according to gospel values which place
love of God and neighbor at the heart of married life,
the couple faithfully responds to their vocation to be
church, to be a healthy and nurturing basis for the
foundational church that is their family as a whole.

Chapter 5

THE SEXUAL, SPIRITUAL FAMILY

WE are sexual beings; from his or her basic genetic structure each person is either male or female, and our sexuality radically conditions our entire being. Each thought, word, and action is that of a male or a female person. It is impossible to be in the world except in a sexual way.

At its most fundamental, our sexuality constitutes our capacity to be in relationship with other persons in more than a superficial fashion. It is our sexuality which enables us to be caring, other-centered, loving people. The man or woman who is psychologically or emotionally alienated from his or her sexuality is handicapped in the pursuit of human intimacy. Thus, if we learn as children that our genitals are "dirty," and bodily pleasure is something to feel guilty about, we are crippled in our ability to be warm and loving with other people. On the other hand, a high level of comfort with our sexuality and with our body in general contributes much to our ability to be in relationships with others successfully.

Even our relationship with God is sexual—at least from the human side. God, of course, is "Person" in ways that transcend sexuality. Yet all the same, by way of the analogies of religious language, God is both female and male. Words of that brief pope, John Paul I, are relevant: "God is a Father, but even more a Mother." Apart from schizophrenia, we cannot set aside our sexuality, either in our relationships with other men and women, or in our relationship with the divine.

Sexuality has a profound impact on family relationships, on the ways we understand our roles in the family, and on the ways in which we communicate Christ to one another. On the most basic level of our sexuality, the family is a complex network of sexual relationships which, when examined from the perspectives of the Judeo-Christian tradition, reveals to us the presence of the Creator in whose image we are created.

Maleness and femaleness, then, is much more than biology. It is more than a psychic reality. It is also that dimension of the person which Yahweh in the Book of Genesis calls "very good." The implications of our sexuality for the life and spirituality of a family *ecclesia* are important ones. For it is the mystery at the roots of human sexuality which draws a man and a woman together. It is this mystery which is the orgin of their faithfulness to one another in love and which enables husband and wife to not only witness but participate in the making of babies and in the years-long process of giving birth to new human persons. It is sexuality which remains the source of the bond between spouses, and it is sexuality—the capacity to touch others in love—which draws the young gradually away from their family of origin into the formation of new loving relationships and new families of their own. If it were not for human sexuality, none of this would happen, except perhaps as it happens for cats, monkeys, and birds.

What does it mean to be a woman? What does it mean to be a man? How can male and female persons be in relationship with one another in ways that are most fully human? How can men and women be in relationship with members of their same sex in ways that do justice to the human mystery? If we are to begin to understand the role of human sexuality in the spirituality of a family, questions like these are of basic importance—because love for one another is central to the purpose of a family's existence and central to the Christian meaning of life. Let us begin to do this, if only in an incomplete way.

Nothing has had so profound an effect on the self-awareness of both women and men in the final decades of the twentieth century as the movement among women to transcend the ways in which society, culture, and history have defined women and their roles. Some activists in the women's movement have formulated goals that not many can agree with. But in great part the women's movement has led in directions which are having beneficial effects on the lives of women, men, and society as a whole.

Families are in a position to benefit from female and male images which are developing as a result of the women's movement. Christian families in particular may benefit from these new images because on a practical level they can help family members relate to one another in ways consistent with the spirit of the gospel, and with the teachings of both the Hebrew and Christian Scriptures. Christian feminist scholars have presented ample evidence of the fact that Christian feminism and Catholicism can benefit from a dialogue based on mutual respect. Thus, a critical listening to the women's movement from a Christian perspective can greatly enrich the life of a Christian family.

Down through the centuries there is probably no institution with which women have been so closely associated as the family in its various forms. And yet the specific ways in which we have come to view this association are no older than the Industrial Revolution. Prior to the emergence of the assembly line, "sweat shops," and white and blue collar work, the place of women in families was far different from what it was by the time today's young adult was chewing bubble gum or buying records by the Beatles. The radical division of roles and labor between the home and the workplace had not occurred. Home and workplace—usually a family farm—were for most people one and the same.

With the triumph of the industrial system, however, factories and offices enjoyed great social status, as places where money was earned, while the home and the women who found themselves assigned there, were devalued in the extreme. A "cult of domesticity" developed which was meant to salve the smarting self-image of wives and mothers, and provide justification for male abandonment of home, hearth, and family for the rigors of "the world." The "cult of domesticity" glorified the home, maternity, and "wifely duties" in a world where everyone knew that what *really* mattered was going on in the factories and other workplaces dominated by men. Although male hats might be symbolically removed at the mention of home, mother, and apple pie, those same hats would go back on as men agreed that "women's work" could not be terribly important. After all, it did not result in money, did it?

Women—confined to their roles as wife and mother—were placed on pedestals on the one hand but were treated like children on the other. Men drew much of their self-esteem from the knowledge that, "My wife will never need to find work outside the home, because I am a good provider." By and large, middle-class women accepted the "cult of domesticity" since it became, in very practical terms, their only source of self-esteem and a very real source of domestic power.

While this sketch depends in great part on mere stereo-typical concepts, still it faithfully reflects the main outlines of the worlds of the majority of men and women not so many years ago.

One of the primary consequences of the women's movement is that more women today view marriage and family as a choice that is open to them but not the only one. No longer is there a quasi-universal sense that the only choices open for Catholic women are marriage and child-rearing or to become a nun. Even when the choice of marriage and family is made—as it still is by most women—few have much sympathy for the belief that a woman can be defined totally in terms of marriage and motherhood. Fewer Catholic women today expect their entire adult life to be taken up by full-time mothering, cooking, cleaning, and doing the laundry, with a bit of volunteer work on the side.

We are at a stage of history, however, where many women who continue to work outside the home after marriage also find themselves with primary responsibility for child care and domestic duties. Many husbands applaud the added income from their wife's job or career but still expect to relax at home while "the little wife" cooks dinner and changes diapers. Thus we have the phenomenon of the woman with two full-time jobs, one as "homemaker" (a euphemism if ever there was one) and another as secretary, waitress, business executive, or bus driver. Some women cooperate with this unfair arrangement for reasons of their own;

others become dissatisfied with it, and a marital crisis
quickly develops.

We must uphold the right of each married couple to
develop together their marital and family roles in ways
best suited for them. But it may be that, in the not-so-
long run, husbands and wives will discover that the
more a relatively equal balance can be worked out, the
more satisfying will their experiences of marriage and
family life become. For many couples, there may be
something unhealthy about marital roles which isolate
husbands and wives from whole areas of one another's
daily life experience.

Ideally, men and women both need to be free to participate in the financial support of the family, and both
need to be free to take responsibility for the physical
maintenance of the home. Both spouses have a right to
participate in the world of the workplace and of secular
society if they so desire. Both can bring the Christian
spirit to this arena in effective ways. Both have a right
to the challenges and satisfaction to be discovered in
nurturing children.

This may indeed be the ideal today. Yet relatively few
couples find it possible to strike such a bargain of a
balance as they would like. Many employers resist arrangements which would free spouses to share careers
or jobs and domestic and parenting duties on a fifty-
fifty basis. (This is but one way in which the lip service
given to family life by politicians at election time, and
corporate employers whenever convenient, is revealed
to be the empty talk it really is.) Many men still object to
abandoning their (now illusory) role as "breadwinner,"
and many women cling to an image of themselves as
"queen of the kitchen," even though they, too, work

outside the home and "win" about as much "bread" as
their husband. But this is a transitional situation which
may not last long.

The future may well see more and more families
whose life will be characterized by a more-or-less equal
sharing of roles, both inside and outside the family circle. Regardless of the specific arrangements worked
out by individual couples, new meanings will gradually
be discovered in the words of St. Paul to the effect that
in Christ there is no male and no female, only the
gospel to be lived and proclaimed by all. And this will
lead to healthier marraiges and happier families.

Moving toward this more balanced sharing of life
responsibilities may become a vital element in a marital
spirituality. Couples who have already taken steps in
this direction readily admit that they are happy with
sharing financial and domestic duties equally, and that
this has had a positive effect on their marriage, as well
as on their effectiveness as parents. One wife commented: "Our marriage is better in every way. We
understand one another's joys and problems, both at
home and in our jobs, because we've both been there.
We both feel that our need for work outside the home
and our desire to be with the children and to putter
around the house are being met in a balanced way. We
now have a happier sex life, too. And our kids like having more equal time with each of us."

To overcome outmoded prejudices about men's and
women's roles requires courage and the willingness to
trust that can come, for Christian men and women,
from a lively faith. Faith comes to life through real risks
taken with our spouse, with our sense of self, and with
our expectations of married life and parenthood. This

is one way in which a spirituality for married people jumps the gap from theory to real life.

Men, of course, often find themselves presented with unique challenges in the midst of society's questioning of traditional roles in families. What does it mean to be a man, a father, a husband? These are questions easily answered thirty years ago, but even those men who cling to the old answers can do so only under siege.

Psychologists tell us that both men and women have a "male" and a "female" side. Women, in order to be most fully what God created them to be, will sometimes act in what are typically recognized as "male" ways. Men, to be all God intended them to be, will sometimes be receptive and nurturant—behaviors traditionally identified with women. Yet women will be "masculine" in a feminine fashion, and men will nurture children and caress their wife, will let the "feminine" side of themselves come out, in masculine ways. In other words, the mystery of human sexuality is experienced by both sexes but in distinctive manners.

So one of the great challenges to the modern male is the challenge to regain his "feminine," nurturant, caring, sensitive, compassionate side, where emotions and feelings are accepted right alongside "being rational" and where cuddling a child is as normal a male behavior as being an aggressive—or passive—lover with his wife. For today's "real man," the cultivation of family relationships takes priority over cultivating a wildly successful career. Giving himself to those he loves is more important than giving them an ever more affluent lifestyle.

Underlying the issue of sex roles in marriage and

family life are two distinctive but complementary spiritualities. As mentioned early in this chapter, our sexuality conditions even our relationship with God. And so there is a feminine spirituality and a masculine spirituality: womanly ways of being in the world in a faith context and manly ways of doing the same. Heavily conditioned by society and culture though these are, they are nevertheless important to be aware of, to encourage, reform, and shape in ourselves according to the spirit of the gospel. Let us examine some of the possible characteristics of these male and female spiritualities.

A woman's spirituality is strong, resilient, and practical. It is rooted in the earth and in a natural communion with the One who gave birth to creation in the beginning and who nurtures it into existence during every moment of time. A woman's spirituality is interior and receptive, being open to the lover God in those she cares for and in the contemplative mystery of conception, pregnancy, and birth. Yet this female spirituality clings fiercely to the God to whom it is open and receptive and will not let go until it is graced by the divine power, though it take the patience of Job.

A woman's prayer is never cold; always it is passionate, even when it is dry or seems to echo with only a great Absence. This is a spirituality familiar with the need to labor by cooperating with the Creator's labors in a woman's life and in the lives of those she loves. A woman often knows, well, yes, intuitively, when in life to get out of the way of the Divine as it labors and when to get in and push, push—even if it means getting pushy with God, insisting that God *do something*.

A woman's spirituality sees signs of God in human

emotions and almost naturally employs the nurturing, empathetic, relational qualities with which a woman is gifted. A woman's spirituality may easily grasp the importance of bringing precisely these qualities into the world of the workplace, and the world of the church, dominated these many, many years by a "masculine" spirit out of touch with its own "feminine" dimensions.

What of a masculine spirituality? It is insistent but gentle, in love with the lover God as a man with a maid. The male spirituality marches up to the dwelling-place of God and bangs on the door when the lives of those a man loves are at stake. A male spirituality is contemplative in its activism. It knows that its roots are in the world of the family, so this spirituality is oriented toward the building of familial relationships.

A masculine spirituality actively pursues intimacy with wife and children, tosses life in the air like an infant, and plays with the Spirit like a child. A masculine spirituality is full of laughter in the face of an uncertain future and refuses to take Mammon too seriously. The spirituality of a Christian man understands that work has value in itself but that work, in the end, is for life, not the other way around. A masculine spirituality brings a Godly spirit to the world of jobs and careers.

A masculine spirituality is modest and shy of self-righteousness. It rejoices in the beauty of the feminine but says, "I pass," when the world would make of women mere objects. Because, this spirituality knows, to do so is to deal a wicked blow to the integrity of self and to the goodness of the Creator of women and men.

If these feminine and masculine spiritualities look as if they are not so distinctive after all, that is because they overlap and regularly commune one with the other. This is another characteristic of both: They seek one another out in order to be complete. Each drinks from the well of the other.

Have we strayed from our theme of family spirituality, of ways for the domestic church to live according to the gospel in the modern world? Not at all. For an essential element of family life is its role in forming men who are genuinely masculine and women who accept and celebrate their femininity in all its dimensions. A family spirituality includes the discipline of enabling husbands, wives, girls and boys, single mothers and fathers, to live as the fully sexual beings God thinks it is good for them to be. And so in our family we respect and rejoice in maleness and femaleness to the point that sometimes we seem to take sexuality for granted. We don't pretend that human sexuality is unimportant or the ultimate fact of life. Neither do we suggest, by word or deed, that human sexuality or the human body are to be avoided or feared. Human sexuality is to be laughed about as often as it is spoken of with a straight face. In the family we learn that through our sexuality—the gift of being able to care for and love others, the gift of being able to bring others into the comedy, the tragedy, the grand party that is life—we are constituted as family. Because of our sexuality we can be faithful in our love for one another and in our love for God who is lover to us all.

Chapter 6

CHRISTIAN PARENTING

IN virtue of their baptism, all Christians are called to ministry, that is, to gift others with the compassion, care, understanding, and joy of the risen Christ. Each is commissioned by Christ to bring the love of God to others in tangible ways.

But we live in a world that frequently discourages the kinds of relationships between people that Christian ministry is all about. More specifically, very often the world of the workplace urges people to look at one another as objects, while those who are parents are expected to be warm and caring at home.

Many people today sense a disparity between their understanding of themselves as disciples of Christ sent to minister to others, and their experience of a highly technologized and very impersonal workplace. Not infrequently today, women and men work at jobs which result in their feeling like little more than extensions of a mechanical or electronic monster. The sense of alienation such people feel in relationship to their jobs is intense. It is such people who make up the rather high percentage of the workforce in some areas of the marketplace who turn to drugs—including marijuana and alcohol—to help ease the experience of meaninglessness.

One example is provided by a young woman we know who works as an Information Operator for a telephone company. Every minute of this young woman's on-the-job time is taken up with providing anonymous voices in her headset with telephone numbers. Not only that, but the company this woman works for urges its Information Operators to keep their discussions with callers as brief as possible. Our friend's average contact with a customer is twenty-seven seconds, but the company encourages her to get her average time down to twenty-five seconds. The ideal seems to be for the Operator to become as "efficient" as the computer on which he or she punches buttons in order to locate telephone numbers for callers. Heaven forbid that the Operator should encourage any kind of—even brief—warm human interaction. No. The ideal is to function with mechanical efficiency, even in contacts with human beings rather than computers.

This is only one example. Many others exist. But the problem is the same: Human relationships and personal forms of interaction are not valued. Even a company which proselytizes its customers to "reach out and touch someone" preaches the exact opposite to its employees.

What does all this have to do with Christian parenting? It illustrates two sides of the same coin. First, we live in a world that does not truly value interpersonal relationships. Second, this is the world in which Christian parents are called to nurture their children. This is the world many parents must live with during the many hours they work outside the home. This workaday world does have an effect on our attitudes toward one another, even in our families.

Parents need to be aware of the ways in which human relationships during work hours may be carried over to relationships in the family. Then we can support efforts to humanize the workplace as well as being cautious about allowing attitudes endorsed by employers about human relationships to dictate our attitudes toward relationships in the family. Through our family relationships we can remain sensitive to the need for warmth in human interaction, to the need to avoid treating others—even over the phone—as objects.

It is within this social context that Christian parents are called to care for and guide their children. It is in this world that parents are called, in fact, to be the pastors of the foundational church that is their family. The world does little to make the ministry of parents any easier. But parents can be aware of exactly what kinds of "games" their society asks them to play. On the one hand, they can resist those "games" which would dehumanize family relationships. On the other, they can dedicate themselves to positive efforts toward helping children learn to be critical of such secular attitudes toward human relationships as we have examined above.

Perhaps the main characteristic of Christian parenting is the understanding on the part of parents that it is in a faith context that they are called to parent. Many of the forms of knowledge and the skills that are helpful to any parent are equally helpful to Christian parents. Christian parents have no magic formulas for raising children, no easy ways out of the tight spots all parents find themselves in with their youngsters from time to time. That which especially characterizes the Christian parent is the religious values background that provides a basis for the minor and major decisions that parents must make regularly.

One of the consequences of this faith context is the way in which the child is viewed by the parent. Most basically, the child is understood to be free, a gift, and a child of God. Let's examine each of these ideas separately.

The child is understood to be free. What is of major interest here is the way in which parents understand the nature of their relationship with the child. A more conventional way of approaching this issue would be to raise the topic of parental authority. What exactly is the nature of the authority parents have with respect to their children? The authors of *An American Catechism* respond this way: "Parents have the authority in the family, but it is an authority whose proper goal is not to demand submission, but to be a guidance toward independence." (Seabury Press)

The child is free. It is the task of parents to guide the young person as he or she develops and help him or her learn to exercise that freedom responsibly. An earlier generation tended to conceive of parental authority as meaning that when Dad or Mom commanded, children were to obey, whether they liked it or not.

Today, as the authors of the catechism quoted above suggest, it seems more appropriate to think of the task of parents as that of helping children learn to make choices and decisions of their own and of being with the child through the consequences which follow, be they pleasant or unpleasant. This is one of the most important ways parents can provide "guidance toward independence."

As with most aspects of parenting, it is our feelings and attitudes as parents that require attention first. Instead of looking at the child first, parents need to ask *themselves* some basic questions throughout the child-rearing years: Am I willing to facilitate my child's growth toward independence in reality and not just in words? Or do I only grudgingly give up the power to control my child's life? Who am I protecting? Sometimes parents say they are trying to protect their children from serious mistakes when in reality they are doing all they can to protect *themselves* from the possible pain of watching their child suffer the sometimes cruel blows life can inflict, but which are often necessary for learning to take place.

Christian parents minister to their children by nourishing in them real growth in their independence or freedom as children of God. In this way, they acknowledge the second aspect of the child's identity: the child as gift.

In most families, the birth of a child happens so easily, so naturally, that the whole process of pregnancy and birth is accepted with hardly a second thought. It is easy to miss the sense of the child as gift, especially once the novelty of having a new baby around the house wears off.

Bur our children are unique gifts of God. They are sent to us, each as different from one another as are the snowflakes. Indeed, our children are sent, each in his or her own way, to minister *to us*. It has been said that children make grown-ups of their parents. It is surely true that it is because of our children that we have the opportunity daily to do some maturing. This is one way of viewing the parenting task as a whole: If we do some growing up, so will our children. If we learn how to better live our lives, how to more faithfully follow Christ, how to more effectively respond to our children, then they, too, will grow up.

Our children are sent to help facilitate our growth as human beings. What we sometimes forget is that from the Christian perspective we experience self-fulfillment only by paradox. It is through death that we live, through what may seem like misery today that we know fulfillment tomorrow.

We sometimes feel sorry for ourselves. "Why have I been sent these kids who cause me so much anxiety, irritation, and trouble? Poor me." But in a very real sense, kids are only carrying out the commission (albeit unknowingly) given them by God. As an eleven-year-old boy remarked to his father, "Dad, don't you know that one of the reasons I'm here is to give you a bad time?"

Here we touch on an important aspect of a spirituality of parenting. Children—there is no getting around it—are one form the cross takes in the lives of parents. Because of children we have specific opportunities daily to die to selfishness, to sacrifice our most cherished prejudices, to set aside our preferences, and to ignore opportunities to coddle our own egos.

No monk rising from his bed of straw in the darkness of night for prayers has more chances for dying to selfishness than parents who rise in the night to care for a hungry or fussy baby or a child who is sick. This is dying to self for love of one's neighbor. No ascetic practices of fasting and penitence embraced by the saints of old were more valuable in the eyes of God as ways of growing in love than the sacrifices made by parents to be able to spend more time with their children or to be able to provide them with enough food or good schooling. The parent who struggles to keep an open mind about his or her teenager's tastes in music and clothing strives to love in ways that cannot be measured. The parent who trusts a child a little more this year than last, and lives with the anxiety that comes with letting go just a little bit more, is attempting to grow in his or her trust in God in ways that cannot be matched.

Third, the child is a child of God before he or she is a child of ours. Underlying the commitment to guide the child toward a responsible exercise of freedom, toward independence, is the firm belief that in the long run the child is in God's hand, not ours. This is to assent to the truth that this child is a mystery—known to us somewhat; known to himself or herself but finally known fully only to God. What greater cause for confidence, for hope, and for feeling okay about letting the child gradually grow up and away?

All that has been said so far can be examined from the perspective of a traditional theological principle which states, "Grace builds on nature." Parents need to gain the practical forms of knowledge and the skills needed to be effective parents in today's world. On the "natural" level—prior to any consideration of religious aspects of parenting—parents need to know their business. They need to read the books of the parenting experts, attend parenting classes, join parent support groups. All of this amounts to gaining practical ministerial skills. For all that the Christian parent gains in the way of practical knowledge and skills becomes so many ways of showing God's love to the child in ways the child can feel. In these ways, love becomes real, not a matter of mere words and fond aspirations. As we relate to our children in the loving ways we learn, we observe in our own actions illustrations of how God loves us.

Parents can learn much about the love of God by paying attention to their own love for their children. Think of your own best moments of love for your offspring. That is but a shadow of how God loves you. Think of the times you let the child fall—literally or figuratively—in order to learn to walk. That is how God allows you to suffer a bit in order to grow stronger in spirit. Consider your feelings of pride and joy when your children have been especially delightful. Just so is God's joy in your existence, your mere presence in the world of his creation. This, too, is an aspect of a spirituality for parents.

Then there are the practical issues that fill a parent's days. To pick but two, let's examine the parent as educator in human sexuality and the parent as religious educator.

As with every aspect of parenting, the parent is most effective in these areas if he or she has gained a balanced and mature integration of sexuality and of faith in his or her own daily existence.

Children begin learning about their sexuality and about relationships with members of the same and opposite sexes from the moment of birth. The baby that is fondled and caressed learns to relax and be comfortable with his or her body. The baby who has his or her hand regularly slapped when it happens to stray into exploration of his or her genitals will more likely have inappropriate feelings about sex to overcome in later years. The child who witnesses his or her parents expressing warmth and affection for one another in physical ways—hugs, kisses, caresses—will feel loved because he or she is confident of living in a loving atmosphere. Such a child will also learn that physical expressions of love and affection are not only appropriate but to be rejoiced in.

Education in human sexuality and religious education have much in common. Both are—in the now
widely used phrase—"more caught than taught." Kids
pick up almost with the air they breathe their parents'
feelings and attitudes toward human sexuality. The
same goes for religion and for the living of one's faith in
daily life. Kids know when religion is little more than a
formal exercise to be endured on Saturday evening or
Sunday morning, even if parents never come right out
and say so. Children also have a kind of sixth sense
when it comes to parental attitudes which make of faith
little more than a psychological security blanket, instead of a constant challenge to take real risks based
on faith and to embrace the cross on a daily basis, in all
kinds of ways, for love of God and other people. Kids
have an uncanny ability to recognize when parents are
merely playing games with religion. They can spot
phoniness in faith a mile away. They can also recognize
authentic faith the minute they see it being lived in concrete ways. Phony faith kids reject on the spot; authentic faith they are naturally attracted to.

As religious educators, it is not the task of parents
first of all to trot out religion books once a week and sit
down with the kids to drill them. Neither is it their first
obligation to enroll the children in a Catholic school or
CCD program—worthwhile though either of these actions may be. Instead, it is the most basic responsibility
of parents to do all they can to be continually growing
and maturing in faith themselves. Do I look at daily life
above all from the perspectives of the gospel or from
the perspectives of the stock market? Do I value the
opinions of Madison Avenue more or those of
respected teachers in the Christian community? Do I

make regular efforts to grow in my understanding of my faith? Do I continue to include personal prayer in my day? Do we as parents cooperate in our efforts to help our children learn about and live the Christian faith?

What about our attitudes toward our relationships with our children? We may say that spending time with our kids is more important than buying them the latest styles in clothing and the toys and games that are currently being "hyped" on television. We may say that our children are more important to us than our jobs or careers, more important than our hobbies. But is this so? One of the best ways to take a look at where our values really are is to look at our calendar and at our checkbook. Where do we spend our time and money? Do we spend more time making money in order to buy *things* for our kids than we spend simply being with them? Do we have a tendency to buy things for our kids to compensate for our failures to share *ourselves* with them?

When was the last time we took a financial risk for the sake of some enjoyable family time together? Oh, it is relatively easy to take a risk when a *necessity* is at stake—food, clothing, the rent, etc. But what about taking financial risks for the sake of what is equally important—collecting memories we can share as a family, memories that will bind us together?

Irish political activist Bernadette Devlin writes, in her autobiography *The Price of My Soul*, that she could always tell as a child when her parents were about to do something for family time together that they couldn't afford. She would hear them saying, "There'll be days when we'll be dead." Bernadette always knew that they

were about to take a family vacation or weekend trip
together for which there was no money. But her
parents valued the short time of their life together more
than possible—even likely—financial shortages.
Somehow the money would work itself out. And it
always did. Bernadette Devlin's parents believed in taking risks in order to put first things first.

Another aspect of sharing faith with our children that
is frequently overlooked is that of introducing our kids
to the whole church. Most kids grow up thinking that
their parish church is just about all there is to being
Catholic. Thus, they may never have a chance to experience the rich variety that is the patchwork quilt of
Catholicism. Kids as they are growing up need to see up
close a Catholic Worker house of hospitality. They
need to have the opportunity to spend some time
around a Trappist monastery. The child's perspective
on the church can broaden considerably by attending
Mass at various ethnic parishes. The sense of faith
comes across in different ways at an inner city parish
pot-luck dinner than it does at a suburban parish picnic. Take them to hear the prayerful chant of a group of
Poor Clare nuns. Introduce them to one of Jean
Vanier's L'Arche houses where emotionally and
physically handicapped persons live together in Christian community. In every part of the country there are
colorful and different ways of living Catholic Christianity going on side by side. Let the kids gain a feel for
what Catholic means: universal. Try to include the
Catholic "sights" along the way on your summer vacations, too. The U. S. is dotted with Catholic shrines and
points of interest. Make of these stops, not just more
rubber-necking on the part of tourists, but part of an

authentic pilgrimage, an attempt to enrich the faith of your family.

So much of the impact parents have on their children happens through simply living together. One of the most profound forms of education children gain from their parents is the preparation they receive to form families of their own one day. Girls and boys learn how to go about being wives and husbands by the ways they observe their own parents doing this. They learn how to parent by being the subjects of parenting. Of course, none of this amounts to a kind of absolute conditioning process. In later years our offspring can often overcome inadequacies in themselves which may be due to parental blind spots or failures. Nevertheless, it is almost impossible to overemphasize the impact parents have on their children when it comes to preparing them to be spouses and parents themselves in adulthood.

There is so much that can be said about parenting. Shelves and shelves of books on parenting fill libraries and book stores. But when all is said and done, we believe Sidney Callahan states in an excellent and concise fashion the ultimate goal of the Christian parent: "to make our children glad they were born and eager for life." If this objective is kept in mind, no matter what the practical issue at hand, the approach best adopted by parents will become apparent soon. Living out of a faith perspective, the Christian parent is especially well-equipped to accomplish precisely this goal.

Chapter 7

SPIRITUALITY AND THE SINGLE PARENT

THERE are many single-parent families in Catholic parishes today. It is therefore imperative that a book on family spirituality give some attention to the experience of single parents and attempt to reflect on the unique dimensions of a spirituality for the single-parent family. Of course, for many, single parenthood is a phase which may last only a few years, between divorce and remarriage. For others, remarriage may not be a consideration for many years, if at all. Some single parents today eventually link up with another single parent to form the phenomenon of the "blended" family. (This is a form of family which has unique characteristics, needs, and strengths, but which is beyond the scope of the present discussion.)

The single-parent family is a true family and a legitimate form of domestic church. For all the ways in which it is unique, it remains a genuine family, a small cell of Christian life. It is from this fact that the basic principles of a single-parent family spirituality will emerge.

It may be helpful, however, to first examine some of the special characteristics of the single-parent family. Both parent and children have gone through painful disruptions which marked the months, sometimes years, which led to a divorce. The family has survived, though much anguish has been known by both parent and children.

Generally, it takes between two and five years for the

practical and emotional aspects of life to become settled again. Sources of income must be developed, a move to a new house or apartment may be necessary, kids may need to attend different schools. Parent-child relationships must be "redesigned." Raising children as a single parent is very different from doing so in tandem with a spouse.

The single father—usually, though not always, the noncustodial parent—finds himself struggling with a whole new set of difficulties. Often there is the need to pay child support to his former spouse. He may become deeply worried about the religious up-bringing of his children, should his former wife remarry someone who is indifferent or antagonistic to Catholicism. The noncustodial father also typically has more time to become depressed and to "brood." He may suffer from acute loneliness.

In fewer situations, single parenthood is the result of the death of a spouse. In such instances, the grieving process unique to this set of circumstances goes on for many months. Yet, as one divorced woman pointed out, the single parent who has been widowed has something going for him or her that the divorced person usually does not. The widowed parent tends to be looked upon by the wider community as courageous, as one who is "slugging it out through thick and thin," after the tragic death of a beloved spouse.

Even today, the divorced Catholic parent tends to be viewed with suspicion. In some parishes the single parent who is divorced often feels shunned, ignored, even subtly ostracized. Yet divorced single parents have a deep desire to belong, to be a part of their church and their parish. Single parents have a need for sympathetic friends and for warm relationships with "normal" two-parent families.

In the great majority of cases, the single parent is a woman. Usually she is divorced, although there is quite an increase in the number of young women who, after becoming pregnant while single, choose to raise their child as a single parent rather than place the child with an adoption agency. But in either case, the fact of being a single *woman* with family responsibilities is often seen as a handicap in our society. Women are not generally paid as well as men for similar work. They also tend to have a more difficult time finding jobs that pay well in the first place.

The single parent, whether male or female, might be most accurately described as a "survivor." Yet she or he is frequently not sure that the survival is going to last until the end of the week. All day long the single parent responds to the demands of either children or employer. And, she or he does it *alone*. If the single parent is lucky, there is an hour or two left over at the end of the day, after the kids are asleep, when she or he can simply sit down and relax—or perhaps "collapse and relax" would be more accurate. This block of time, if the single parent is fortunate enough to have it, becomes critically important time to maintain some degree of emotional and psychological stability.

Weekends, for the single-parent family even more than for the two-parent family, are times for "catching up"—catching up with the housework, catching up with shopping for groceries, and taking care of errands that won't get done any other time. Of course, the single parent may be required to work on weekends, in

which case matters are further complicated by the
disparity between the parent's schedule and that of the
kids who are still in school. There is also the question of
care for children during the summer when the parent
must continue to work but school is out.

Perhaps the majority of single-parent families must
constantly struggle with financial anxieties. Even if an
absent father pays child support, the shift from being a
two-income, or one male income, household, to a one
(usually female) income household, is typically
traumatic. Many college-educated single mothers find
themselves seeking help from county or state agencies.

Probably the best word to describe the condition of
the single parent is "tired." One single mother of two
preschool age children remarked: "I seem to be ex-
hausted all the time, I never really seem to feel rested
and relaxed. There just isn't time for that because it's
push-push-push, all day long, every day." Again, the
main difference for the single parent comes from having to cope *alone*. Sure, married parents get tired, too.
But there is something about being tired *with* another
adult that makes it, by comparison, that much more
bearable. In a two-parent family, Dad can take the kids
to the park for the afternoon so Mom can relax for a
couple of hours. In the single-parent family it just isn't
that simple.

Most single parents find that because they must give
virtually all of their time to children and "bringing
home the bacon," there is little time left over for keeping a clean and tidy house. Even those who consider
themselves incapable of living in "a messy house," do
learn to live with the mess. It's unavoidable. One
mother commented: "When you're a single parent

something has to go, and it's usually the upkeep of the house."

Yet, with all the time that must be given to caring for children, most of it involves taking care of essentials—preparing meals, helping with homework, getting them off to school in the morning and into bed at night. Single parents tend to feel guilty about not spending enough "quality" time with their kids. In a two-parent family, on Saturday Dad can prepare lunch while Mom reads the little ones a story, or "shoots the breeze" with older kids. In the single-parent family, if Mom is fixing dinner, that's it; there is no one free to read a story or simply listen to how school went that day. Mom is responsible for everything, but everything is not about to get done.

One of the deepest pains experienced by the single parent is the knowledge that, in the words of another single mother, "My children will never fully understand what a real Christian family is because they will never have witnessed a normal man/woman, husband/wife loving relationship. This leaves a great void in our life as a family, I think, and this is the one thing, as a single parent, that I cannot give my kids."

The single parent tends to operate at peak energy expenditure levels day in, day out. Still, now and then a single parent will decide that she or he is going to be "super parent" all the same, that "my kids aren't going to have it any different from other kids." Such a parent, in the words of a single father, "is setting himself up for two or three ulcers and a one-way ticket to the looney bin." The single parent family *is* different, and, as we shall see, accepting this fact is one element of a single parent's spirituality.

There are, of course, some positive aspects to the experience of the single parent. There is something to be said for being a "survivor." Just "making it" is something to be proud of. In a society which tends to produce high-school graduates who have never been required to take on responsibility for much more than school studies and maybe a part-time job, the children of single-parent families have often found it necessary to grow up more rapidly. Such kids are sometimes more mature than many of their peers from two-parent families. They have, of necessity, been trusted with significant responsibilities at home—perhaps everything from getting meals ready on time to shopping for their own clothes on a limited budget; from caring for younger siblings to making sure the car gets oil changes on schedule. In some instances, kids have found it necessary to find part-time jobs, not to fund cars and stereo systems, but to contribute much-needed money to the family income.

Granted the incomplete character of this description of the single-parent family, nevertheless it communicates the general outlines of a single-parent family's experience of life. It is the real world of the single parent that is of prime importance if we are to reflect on the unique aspects of a spirituality for these often courageous and deeply Christian families. For, as we have said, an authentic Christian spirituality takes the real experience of real people and brings it into an intimate relationship with the Spirit and gospel of Jesus Christ.

A spirituality for the single-parent family does not lead off into some dream world where there will be "pie in the sky by and by." Rather, it turns the single

parent around to face the realities of her or his life
squarely. This spirituality then enables the single
parent to cope with these realities from a faith perspective—that is, from the perspective of a personal relationship with Christ. The single parent who strives to
be a friend and follower of Christ confronts the same
facts of life as any single parent. But she or he does so,
or tries to do so, according to the perspectives of the
gospel. It is this which makes all the difference.

The single-parent family stands challenged by the
same gospel which is addressed to all. But it is within
the unique circumstances of the single-parent family
that a response is called for. The single parent is invited
to conversion of heart and life, to trust God above all, to
abandon fear, to love God and others as the source of
life's meaning and purpose. The single parent is called
to do this even in the midst of meaninglessness and the
temptation to despair.

As church, the single-parent family can cultivate
prayer and family rituals, can know forgiveness and
reconciliation, can cultivate a life of service, participate
in a parish community, and proclaim the gospel effectively. If anything, the single parent may be more free
to lead her or his children in this way of life. In two-
parent families value conflicts which relate to the
spiritual life of the family can sometimes develop between husband and wife. Or one parent may choose to
be a "noncooperator" with regard to fashioning the life
of the family along explicitly Christian lines. The single
parent, on the other hand, is quite free to provide
religious leadership without possible hinderance from
a reluctant spouse. The main prerequisite is the decision to live the life of a single-parent family according
to the spirit of the gospel.

Two of the major obstacles to making a decision in favor of the gospel as primary inspiration and guide for the single-parent family are the temptations to self-pity and resentment. The gospel challenges the single parent to leave self-pity and resentment behind. Support groups for single parents can be very helpful in the effort to overcome these self-defeating behaviors.

The difficulties unique to the experience of the single parent are very real. But any life involves suffering. Every Christian is called to shoulder the cross in various ways, for it is only by doing so that authentic resurrection will ever be known, in this life or the next.

Okay, so we are a single-parent family. We can still be together each evening for dinner; we can still join hands around our table for prayer. All it takes is the decision to try. We can still live our life together according to our faith in Jesus Christ and strive to ignore the phony gods of a secularized society. All it takes is the ongoing decision to try to do so.

All families know insecurity. However, perhaps the single-parent family is privy to forms of fear and anxiety that other families do not usually know with such intensity. Financial anxieties may head the list, but a vague, undefined fear of what the future may bring is not far behind. The single parent is unable to share these fears and anxieties with another intimately known adult, and she or he lives with these feelings constantly. So the fear tends to compound itself. But, like all families, the single-parent family is called to turn away from fear and anxiety as motives for action. In ways characteristic of the single-parent family, the single parent can know that out of dying to such fears even now can come eternal life. Words of Jesus take on a special meaning for the single parent who may be anxious or fearful: "Fear is useless, what is needed is trust" (Mk. 5:36) When problems continue to pile up, it is at this point that the single parent can learn to let go and trust in God from deep within herself or himself.

In the two-parent family, it is crucial for spouses to spend time regularly on themselves and on their friendship as a couple. It is equally important for the single parent, "by hook or by crook," to carve out of the week a few hours for leisure and, now and then, for prayerful reflection. Single parents may support one another in this. You take my kids on Saturday morning, I'll take yours on Sunday afternoon. Sometimes if the single parent's own parents or siblings live nearby, they can be of invaluable assistance in helping her or him to have some regular leisure time. Two-parent families who are friends of the single-parent family are perhaps especially gifted to share their relative stability and strength by offering supplemental child care now and then.

The single parent often finds it necessary to struggle against the tendency to become isolated. Parish community and support groups for divorced Catholics and single parents can be helpful. Isolation has its own unique dangers for the single-parent family, including the inclination to "make mountains out of mole-hills." That is, relatively minor difficulties can grow in the imagination until they seem completely overwhelming. Single parents often need nothing more than a sympathetic listener, and they can frequently find this by forming friendships with other single parents, and by membership in parish family groups. To have close relationships with "normal" two-parent families is often of special importance. Sadly, many parishes have still not grown to the point where family groups exist, and when they do they are often at loose ends when it comes to welcoming single-parent families into their midst.

Continued faith in God that makes a real difference in how life is lived and continued faith in oneself and in one's essential goodness constitute a constant struggle for many single parents who are divorced. To go on believing that God's love is at work in my life as a single parent, and in our family relationships, is rarely easy. But it is vital to keep on trying. A basic principle for a single parent's spirituality: "Keep on keeping on."

The single parent who is widowed may recall that in the New Testament we have witness to the compassionate love of Christ for the suffering of a widowed parent. Note that Jesus reaches out to help the woman without being asked to do so. (Perhaps the woman's grief was so intense that she didn't even know Jesus was there.)

> As [Jesus] approached the gate of the town a dead man was being carried out, the only son of a widowed mother.... The Lord was moved to pity upon seeing her and said to her, "Do not cry" (Luke 7:11-13).

Jesus looks with love on the pain of the widowed parent and spontaneously reaches out to help. "Do not cry," he says, before bringing the son back to life. Yet it is so easy for single parents, widowed or divorced, to disbelieve this love in their own life, to act as if she or he must "do it all alone." Yet even when parish communities which should be more supportive and caring are not, the single parent is never alone. The caring and

powerful love of God *is* there, and the members of the
family have been given to one another as signs of love
by a loving God. Christ extends his hand and invites the
single parent to trust, even to trust blindly.

In the midst of our discussion, we must still be on the
offensive against misunderstanding, particularly when
it comes to the use of the term "spirituality." For the
single parent, too, there is sometimes the feeling that
spirituality is a luxury for which she or he has no time.
The assumption here is that "spirituality" is an activity
one engages in during times which are set apart from
ordinary life, or perhaps it is a set of emotions one
cultivates in order to "feel spiritual."

We must repeat that spirituality, even for the single
parent, refers first to the ways we strive to go about
"being in the world." Spirituality refers to a decision,
or set of decisions, about how we will live and the ways
we try to follow through on these decisions. The values,
standards, and goals we embrace are at the very heart
of our spirituality—the "whys" behind the way we live
and the things we do. Thus, the single Christian parent
chooses to be "led by the Spirit," rather than being led
around by the nose by self-pity or resentment.

Perhaps the major influence which shapes any single
parent's spirituality is the fact that the deepest bond
she or he knew in life has been severed, through
divorce or death. So there is the need to refashion a
bond with God, the source of a love which is perfectly
trustworthy and always there.

The single parent, even in minor matters, must make
decisions about the lives of her or his children which
demand a great deal of trust in God. Should I allow my
daughter to attend a slumber party? Is she old enough?

To make such a seemingly ordinary decision can be anxiety-inducing in the extreme when it must be made alone. An important element in a single parent's spirituality is cultivation of the ability to be honest with one's children about parental anxieties and cultivation of the ability to make decisions trusting that in the end these kids are more in God's hands than mine.

Today single parents are more visible in parishes, and this is right. Single parents who have arrived at a point in their personal life where they are able to do so may discover that a significant aspect of her or his spirituality becomes prophetic in nature. There is a need for single-parent families to be represented on parish committees and advisory groups. The perspectives, needs, and sensitivities of single-parent families deserve to be taken into account on every level of parish life, from the rectory to the committee charged with responsibility for planning the parish picnic. Homilists could often be more sensitive to the realities which characterize the life of single-parent families.

Someone needs to speak up for single-parent families in the parish. Who better than a single parent who can say, "I've paid my dues as a single parent." Such a person knows what it feels like to experience a divorce as a Catholic. She or he has coped with the financial worries, the sexual frustrations, and the spiritual desert unique to the experience of divorce and single parenthood. But often the other side of these experiences has been a growth in compassion for all who suffer and in the freedom to rejoice with those who rejoice. The single parent who has become a deeper, more mature person through her or his experiences is, in other words, a prime candidate for lay ministry in a parish.

The spirituality of the single parent is built around and nourished by the real world of the single-parent family. In some respects this calls forth a unique spirituality. But this spirituality is one which, like any Christian spirituality, brings the single parent and her or his children into communion with God and one another as its primary purpose.

Chapter 8

THE DOMESTIC CHURCH AND THE PARISH CHURCH

A family's spirituality—its dedication to living the Christian life in everyday ways—is affected very heavily by its participation in the life of a parish. So it is important to discuss the relationship between the family and the parish.

When "church" is mentioned, nearly all Catholics think first of their local parish. This is understandable. For as long as anyone alive today can remember, the parish is what we have meant when we say "church." But the rediscovery today is of the simple fact that parish church and domestic church are interdependent. You can't really have one without the other. In his book *Religion: A Secular Theory*, sociologist Father Andrew Greeley states the point concisely: "The family is a more important institution of religious socialization than the church. But, the church is still important."

For many generations, parishes have been able to take families for granted. It could be taken for granted that families would remain basically strong, that familial relationships would, for the most part, weather hard times. Divorce was relatively rare. Families tended to live in places not too distant from grandparents, aunts, uncles, and cousins. It was rarely questioned that family values would be shaped primarily by the Judeo-Christian tradition—if not entirely by the church, at least through the vague but still identifiable and generally accepted manifestation of this tradition in society at large. Parish leaders knew they could

count on Catholic families to support their parish, personally and financially, so prior to twenty years ago
few gave it a second thought. God was in his heaven
and all was more or less right with the world, the
parish, and the family.

But the world changed, families have changed, and
so have parishes. Parish leaders can no longer assume
that families will be more-or-less capable of effectively
nourishing the Christian life in their homes. Many
families are terribly strained, many families break
under the pressure of a secular world. A few years ago,
the Administrative Board of the United States Catholic
Conference pointed out that today's families are
"evangelized" far more effectively by the secular mass
media—most notably television—than by the church.
The life of a typical American Catholic family is im-
pacted far more heavily by the materialism of the
secular world than it is by the gospel of Jesus Christ and
the official teachings of the church. As a result, families
tend to be characterized by a kind of emotional and
spiritual schizophrenia. Many families which still attend Mass most Sundays tend to view their religion as
set apart from the rest of their lives: God is over here on
Sundays (or Saturday evenings) and maybe here for
grace before meals (on those rare occasions when we
sit down to a meal as a family). However, "the real
world" and our real lives take up the far larger chunk of
our time.

The gospel proclaims that authentic human fulfillment and peace are to be found through a radical commitment to God and other people—especially to our
neighbors, those with whom we live most closely.
But—through no fault of their own, really—Catholic

families tend to *live* pretty much like the rest of America lives in the pursuit of more and more of everything: money, possessions, a newer and bigger house, two or three cars, more beautiful landscaping around the house, a boat, a snow blower, two or three television sets, and an automatic garage door opener. Although the gospel proclaims, and the church teaches, that the purpose of life is love of God and neighbor, many mainstream American Catholic families tend to reserve talk about such for inconsequential situations. When the chips are down—as they are nearly every day—life is about the pursuit of emotional satisfaction and security through the accumulation of more money and more of the things that money can buy and there is no such thing as enough.

This is the situation of the parish today: largely missing the boat, because many Catholic families are not vital cells of Christian faith, hope, and love. Because the Christian life is not lived on a daily basis by families *as families*, what goes on in parishes is largely a matter of going through the motions during the week and formal ritualism on the weekends.

This is not meant to imply, of course, that parishes are completely phony. Certainly, much good is done on a one-to-one basis: the sick are visited, certain individuals struggle heroically to make the parish a genuine Christian community. But this usually involves a small minority of people. In most parishes, the great majority of those on the census list are seen only on Sundays and rarely spoken to by anyone else. These are the "anonymous Catholics," who may drop a little or a lot of money in the collection basket but are almost never involved in the parish as a community.

That brings up the crux of the matter. Most parishes are not communities. They are "sacramental service stations," places to turn for nourishment of one's individualistic piety, a place to go, perhaps, when your marriage is on the rocks, a place to send the kids for school or CCD. The parish for many Catholics is for Sunday Mass, for baptisms, weddings, and funerals. For a few today, it is the place for "going to confession." When your life is struck by tragedy, you might visit with a priest—a man you have probably never talked with before on any but a superficial level. But that's about it. Most parishes are not communities. Being Christian is not understood as a commitment to involvement in a community. It is something of a private nature, something you "do" publicly once a week and at times like Christmas and Easter.

What has this long-winded streak of negative talk been for? Simply to illustrate the conviction that, generally speaking, parishes are out of touch with families, and families are out of touch with parishes. Families and parishes need one another if either is to be an authentic form of Christian community life. At this point in history, the ball is in the parish's court. Either parish leaders begin to take serious and effective steps to evangelize families and nourish family life and the Christian life in families, or the day is not too far off when we can kiss the church goodby as a viable institution in the United States.

Most parish renewal programs are based on the assumption—unspoken though it is—that a parish is a gathering of individuals whose relationships with one another are unimportant to what the parish is about. Such programs fail to grasp the vital truth that the most important reality in any individual's life is his or her personal relationships. The most important reality in life is the couple's marriage, relationships between children and parents, the friendship between children and their grandparents—even if the grandparents do live several hundred miles away. It is within the context of close personal relationships that faith is experienced most fundamentally. I cannot separate love of God and love for spouse, children, parents, brothers, and sisters. Parish renewal programs that miss this critical point do little more than stir up the water for a few weeks, because they do not enable people to grow closer to one another and then to see that *this* is where God is.

Very often parish leadership personnel are ill-equipped to understand and nourish families. The idea of family ministry is usually thought to be just another program, something else for the parish calendar, reason to set up another committee. Nothing could be further from the truth. Family ministry is far more than that: it is a whole different way of being a total parish community. Family ministry is first of all a set of values and attitudes that inform and shape every ministry in the parish—from visiting the sick to the parish school or the religious education program for children; from weekend liturgies to the quality of life in the rectory. Family ministry says that all ministries must be relational ministries. In other words, no matter what the situation the central focus must not be on the individual isolated from others; rather, it is a person's intimate relationships that are at the very heart of the situation. You minister to the individual by ministering to his or her relationships with those he or she loves.

You provide baptismal preparation not by handing the parents some facts about baptism and their responsibility for raising the child as a Christian. Instead, you introduce the family as a whole into a more complete participation in the Christian community. If the family is not already participating in a neighborhood family cluster community, you have a representative of that "mini-parish" visit the family in their home to acquaint them with the group's purposes, meeting times, etc. You facilitate the nourishing of the couple's marriage. You nourish relationships in that family in any way you can. In this way, the family is offered opportunities to become better prepared to pass along the Christian tradition to the infant to be baptized.

You do all these things because you have said— perhaps without ever putting it into so many words— that no family can live the Christian life alone, that no family can raise a child as a Christian if that family is isolated from other Christian families.

This illustration implies a very important point. Fundamental to the mission of the parish today is the formation of basic Christian communities within each parish. These family cluster communities need to be based not on a kind of group introversion. They must be based on caring for and serving one another, on growing together in faithfulness to the gospel and to meet catechetical and liturgical needs. In addition, the focus must be on supporting and celebrating one another precisely as families. It must never be forgotten that the most important influence on the faith of the individual in the basic community comes from his/her relationships with those with whom he or she shares life most closely. Marriages need to be sustained and enriched, parents need to be supported, retired couples need to be involved, single people need to be welcomed.

Each family cluster community needs—if it is to survive and thrive—a common form of serving others. There must be a shared commitment to helping engaged couples prepare for marriage, to providing hospitality for the families of prisoners, to working for justice and peace, to looking after elderly persons, to visiting the sick, to a lived compassion for families going through the tragedy of separation or divorce, or struggling with the disease of alcoholism. Why not arrange for the married couples in a basic community to become qualified to serve as paraprofessional marriage counselors? The point is that every basic community must be involved in some form of *shared* service. Some will serve in support roles, others will be involved directly. When all is said and done, it is this shared service to others that bonds families to one another. It is this shared meeting of the needs of others that brings about community.

It becomes the ministry of parish leaders and professionals from diocesan agencies to support the ongoing existence of these basic communities within the parish. The parish staff can become the administrators of such things as a parish referral service. A young woman is in the hospital following a miscarriage. Mrs. Smith can visit her because she has had the same experience, and her husband can visit the woman's husband. Perhaps they can get together as couples.

A family in the parish with teenagers is experiencing a lot of turmoil due to the involvement of one of their children with drugs. Another family that has successfully worked through just this situation can help by listening, by being there, and by sharing their own experiences.

Mr. Johnson's wife died yesterday. Call Mr. Carlson and ask him to go over for awhile to visit with Mr. Johnson, since he lost his wife last year.

One of the most important roles of parish professionals becomes that of facilitating ministries within the parish. Family ministry is not merely professionals "doing unto" families. Perhaps more importantly, it is families ministering to one another in all kinds of ways. The underlying conviction is that families need other families if they are to live the Christian life. Parish professionals can help to make this happen.

Anthropologist Margaret Mead once suggested that governments should be as sensitive to families as they are to the environment. Before a major construction project is begun, an environmental impact study is usually completed to determine how the ecological balance will be affected by the proposed construction. What Dr. Mead suggested was that governments should require that similar studies be made to find out what kinds of civil laws, policies, and programs will have on the lives of families. Do our tax laws, for example, help or hinder healthy marriages? Do the educational policies of our schools contribute to the well-being of families or add to their burdens?

This same approach could be of immense value to parishes that are serious about supporting families as cells of Christian life. Families need to be asked: "How do the programs, services, and policies of our parish affect your life as a family?"

Of course, this question would need to be expressed

in many particular questions to apply to the many specific aspects of parish life. Let's look at a few examples.

In many parishes it is still common for religious education to confine itself to programs that divide families into age groupings, that divide men from women, teenagers from children and adults, and adults from teens and children. (Thus, the family is fractured by the parish instead of being nourished.) One result of this is the traditional CCD program. So let's say that the parish poses the following question to families: "How does our CCD program affect your life as a family?"

More than a few families would have to admit that this approach to religious education for children fails to nourish family life; indeed, that in many cases it has an eroding effect on family relationships. Most CCD programs fail to relate in any significant way to the child's identity as a member of a domestic faith community. Parents and siblings share the child's experience in CCD in nebulous ways, if at all.

The one-hour-per-week approach to religious education for children usually misses completely the fact that family relationships are at the heart of the child's faith-related needs. Moreover, the CCD schedule is usually mismatched to family routines. Once a week Mom or Dad must fit a car trip to the parish facilities into an already busy schedule. Parents in some cases may sit in the parish parking lot while they wait for CCD classes to end. This approach to religious education for children reinforces the idea that parents have little of significance to do with the child's religious formation—in spite of all the words from official church sources about parents being the primary religious educators of their children.

Very possibly, parental responses to this question would lead a parish to reassess the value of current CCD types of programs, if nourishing family life is basic to the mission of the parish.

Another area of concern might be the quality of parish liturgies. The Saturday evening or Sunday morning Mass is the one time of the week in most parishes when the church as institution touches families *as families* in a direct way. So the question would be asked: "Do Sunday Masses nourish your life as a family?" Some parents would say that the opportunity for Sunday Eucharist gives them new strength to commit themselves to building strong family relationships. Others might respond that Sunday Mass is a needed respite from the daily grind.

But how many families' responses would reflect an awareness of the Sunday Eucharist as a celebration of their life as a small Christian community? How many would say that the homilies they hear touch their life as a family and help them to be more faithful to their identity as a domestic church? It might well be that the responses to a question on liturgy would illustrate the need to fashion homilies and Sunday Masses more attuned to the lives of families of all kinds, more sensitive to the place of the family as the foundational church.

Many more specific questions could be formulated on issues that touch both parish life and family life:

"How does the physical arrangement of pews and other furniture in our church affect your experience of liturgy as a family? (Ask the parents of young children *that* one!)

"How does our parish scheduling of evening meetings and educational programs affect your family's time together?"

There are dozens of ways in which parishes touch the lives of families, for good or for ill. So it is critical today for parish leaders to be aware of how their practical decisions help or do not help families.

Personal relationships enter into the picture in other ways, too. The relationships that exist between families and priests are of prime importance. If a parish is to be a family of families, then the parish priest is key. It is essential for priests to accept the many important implications of the truth that the family is the foundational church; that unless the Christian life is lived by families it will not be lived by parishes.

Some priests need to reexamine the kinds of assumptions upon which our understanding of the parish has been based for so long: that the parish is an institution the pastor must keep in existence, primarily by being a manager and fund raiser; that the proper spirituality for a parish is one that is basically individualistic.

It may be difficult at times for a celibate priest to appreciate the role of families in today's church. Sometimes—not inhabiting the same emotional and spiritual world—he doesn't develop an appreciation for the intimate, personal, relationship issues that are of such critical importance to the faith and lives of families. It would be well for such priests to take to heart the observation of Father Alfred McBride that celibacy is meant to be a way of drawing closer to people, not a means for distancing oneself from them.

A first step toward bringing priests into the life of families would be for family people to gently urge their

priests to move from institutional to family ways of
thinking and living. Families may be called today to
reach out to priests, insofar as this is possible, to do
what they can to draw priests into their family lives.
We are not talking about the polite, put-on-your-best-
behavior business of getting out the good tablecloth
because Father is coming over for dinner. Instead,
Father may simply need to be drawn into the everyday
world of diapers and teenagers, the first year of marriage, family squabbles, grandparents, family games
and family prayer—the world of tossing the salad, taking turns, and sharing. We do not mean to over-
simplify here. It is never easy to bring about this kind of
clergy-family sharing. But we must begin and keep on
trying.

Priests sometimes need families that will encourage
them to drop in when the notion strikes, to join them
for dinner at the last minute, to come along for summer
vacations or weekend trips, to leave the Roman collar
in the rectory, to kick off their shoes and just be
themselves—no formal meetings or programs, no agen-
da, no priestly "image" to maintain. When that happens, of course, the priest must be prepared to have his
lap occupied by giggling or tearful little ones; he must
be open to becoming a hugger and tickler of two-year-
olds and a friend of teenagers.

Priests, for their part, can make the rectory a more
family kind of place. One simple idea would be to invite
a different family over for dinner one evening a week.
Make it an informal affair. Give the cook the night off
and make way for Family Night. Father could get Mom
and Dad involved with helping to prepare dinner in the

kitchen. The kids could play outside or inside and not worry about being altogether still and quiet. The parish could invest in a high chair for the rectory dining room for families who have a baby. Get a booster seat or two for toddlers. Then have a good old family dinner, nothing fancy, the primary purpose of which is the nourishment of relationships between priest and family.

Priests have a responsibility to do what they can to help married couples and children feel more comfortable around them. If the priest takes the risks necessary to share his real self and life with married couples, married couples are more likely to feel comfortable sharing themselves and their marriage with him.

When priests share the lives of families and families share the lives of priests, they get to know one another apart from artificial clergy/laity distinctions. You want vocations to the priesthood? You'll get them when kids have a chance to get to know Father as a real person, not just as a distant liturgical functionary or authority figure. You want priests who deliver homilies that make sense to the folks in the pews? You'll get them when Father experiences first-hand how faith is lived, celebrated, and struggled with by families, in their relationships with one another.

Parishes need strong Christian families because without them parishes are empty of life and meaning. Families need parishes, because no family can live the Christian life in isolation. A family may knock itself out trying to be an authentic cell of Christian life, a real domestic church. But if the parish isn't being faithful to its role as a supporter of family life and a convener of groups of families, that family will be greatly handicapped in its efforts to pass along the faith to children and to live that faith authentically in the 1980s. Parishes need families; families need parishes.

Chapter 9

THE FAMILY SPIRIT: IN BUT NOT OF THE WORLD

IN his book *St. Thomas Aquinas: The Dumb Ox*, G. K. Chesterton compared the condition of the Christian in the world to that of a huge old oak tree—roots deep into the earth, yet its topmost branches seem to touch the stars at night. This is also true of the Christian family. As an authentic form of *ecclesia* the family is sent by Christ into the world, to be for the world, to serve and love and care for God's creation and God's people. But at the same time, in the words of the Letter to the Hebrews, the members of the family *ecclesia* acknowledge themselves to be "strangers and foreigners on the earth. . .seeking a homeland."

The existential condition of the Christian family is reflected in the words of the Johannine Christ:

> Father. . .I am in the world no more, but these are in the world. . .they do not belong to the world. . . . I do not ask you to take them out of the world. . . . They are not of the world any more than I belong to the world. As you have sent me into the world, so I have sent them into the world (Jn 17:1-19).

Traditionally, this strain of thought from the Fourth Gospel is summed up by the phrase, "in but not of the world." It is imperative that both the "in" and the "not of" receive equal emphasis.

The so-called Letter to Diognetus, written in the late second or early third century, offers another, more

detailed description of the Christian condition in the
world:

> For Christians cannot be distinguished from the rest of the
> human race by country or language or customs. They do
> not live in cities of their own; they do not use a peculiar
> form of speech; they do not follow an eccentric manner of
> life...they live in Greek and barbarian cities alike...and
> follow the customs of the country in clothing and food and
> other matters of daily living.... They live in their own
> countries, but only as aliens.... Every foreign land is
> their fatherland, and yet for them every fatherland is a
> foreign land.... It is true that they are "in the flesh," but
> they do not live "according to the flesh." They busy
> themselves on earth, but their citizenship is in
> heaven...to put it simply: What the soul is in the body,
> that Christians are in the world. The soul is dispersed
> through all the members of the body, and Christians are
> scattered through all the cities of the world. The soul
> dwells in the body, but does not belong to the body, and
> Christians dwell in the world, but do not belong to the
> world.

In this excerpt from the Letter to Diognetus we must
make allowances for a body/soul dualism which seems
out of place today. All the same, these words illustrate
again that the existential condition of the Christian
family is one of "in but not of the world." Another more
contemporary way to express this same idea would be
to say that the Christian family lives in a counter-
cultural fashion. That is, the family strives to live according to standards and values which are sometimes
at odds with those embraced by the dominant culture.
On the other hand, it is also true that there is much

about secular society in which the Christian family rejoices. So the domestic church/family cannot be said to be in favor of a gloom-and-doom outlook on life simply because it chooses to fashion its life in ways that are counter to some of the dominant trends in society at large. The Christian family is not convinced that the world is going to hell in a handbasket.

Nevertheless, what may be most evident about the spirituality of the Christian family, and the lifestyle which arises from this spirituality, are the ways in which the Christian family may choose to be different. Much about the life of the domestic church/family may be counter-cultural, not in ways that are viewed as negative, but in ways that always make positive statements. In fact, much that has been said about a family spirituality in these pages reflects a counter-cultural stance based on the spirit of the gospel.

We have said that the Christian family places a heavy emphasis on giving regular time to nourish family relationships and encourages its members to spend regular time in prayerful solitude. This is clearly a counter-cultural perspective in a society which values an extreme individualism on the surface, but insists on social conformity when the chips are down. It is also true that in our society "privacy" is valued but prayerful solitude is not.

The Christian family is serious (though not grim!) about a family dedication to serving others who have special needs. This service orientation is counter-cultural in a society which believes in "looking out for Number One" and passing the buck to huge agencies and institutions when it comes to the poor, the underprivileged, the handicapped, and those who are dying of loneliness. There is nothing trendy about a dedication to serving others.

The Christian family, we said, patiently develops ways for prayer and ritual to have a comfortable part in the normal ebb and flow of the family's daily life. This is counter-cultural in a world which would secularize family life right along with every other aspect of society. When has a television sit-com family or "soap opera" family ever been portrayed sharing mealtime prayer (outside of programs where this prayer is presented as merely nostalgic or quaint, e.g., "The Waltons")? Natural family prayer and ritual are counter-cultural in the extreme, for they reflect and nourish the family's relationship with the One who is the source and goal of the family's very existence.

The foundation of the foundational church (in its traditional nuclear form) is the continuing promise of the married couple to remain faithful to one another in love. And so they make the sacrifices necessary to spend time with one another, apart from their children, regularly. This is crazy behavior in a society which views marriage as primarily a legal arrangement, lifelong marriage as a pipe dream, and divorce as the logical outcome of marriage. So the spirituality of the married couple is counter-cultural, too.

We outlined the character of the relationship between the family and the parish and pointed out how important these two forms of church are to one another. This, too, is counter-cultural. We live in a society which encourages families to live isolated from one another. In many parts of the country, the traditional neighborhood and the traditional neighborhood parish are ghosts of the past. To believe in the formation of family communities is to adhere to principles which are counter-cultural.

It has also been noted that spending *time with* children is more important than spending *money on* children. To highlight this attitude as part of Christian parenting is to encourage (at the very least) a lack of support for our economic system, the ultimate principle of which is to buy as much as possible as often as possible—whether you need it or not. Parents are instructed daily by mass media advertising and peer attitudes that giving children things is what the good parent does. To value committed personal relationships over the stockpiling of possessions is highly counter-cultural.

The single-parent family is challenged by and finds comfort in the same gospel with which all are presented. To respond to this gospel in authentically Christian ways will sometimes place the single-parent family at odds with the values and attitudes of the dominant culture.

We have seen ways in which a Christian view of human sexuality has an impact on a family spirituality and on the ways in which husband and wife may understand themselves and their roles. We live in a society which tends to trivialize human sexuality and human relationships. Some very powerful elements in the dominant culture encourage the alienation of men and women from their sexuality. A Christian approach to this dimension of human nature and human existence will often require the Christian family to think and believe in ways which are scorned by a secularized world.

Finally, when we discussed the ways in which the

family proclaims the gospel, we emphasized the need for the family to allow the gospel to condition all aspects of its life. Truly, this is the most basic counter-cultural act. For to live like this is to place the true God above all the phony gods of a secularized culture—including the gods of materialism, violence, profit, and production—while at the same time embracing the good that is there wherever it may be discovered. To do this is to reject the popular conception of religion as "a private matter," which should have nothing significant to do with social or political issues. (Consider, for example, the outrage from some sectors not so long ago when the Catholic bishops of the United States were so bold as to address in the public forum the issue of the nuclear arms race.) The dominant culture views religion as an ho-hum activity to be isolated to Sunday mornings, before big-time sports demand our presence in front of the television screen. Any attempt on the part of religion to violate these boundaries is labeled "religious fanaticism."

It is clear, then, that we have already presented in some detail the counter-cultural character of a Christian family spirituality. Yet there are other consequences of this "in but not of the world" condition that remain to be examined.

The role of television in the life of the domestic church community may require constant vigilance. Many families today are concerned about the impact of television on the quality of family life. Families often find that much of the time they do have together is handed over to watching television. But even if we watch several programs together as a family, our togetherness is superficial. Suggestions from educators that families watch a program together then turn off the set and discuss what they have watched seem naive. How many families find they have the power to turn off the set once it is turned on? It has even been suggested by extensive research that television can become an addictive "drug," so that it no longer matters what is being watched; all that matters is watching. Numerous studies, as well as the experience of many ordinary families, indicate that heavy television watching has destructive effects on parent/child relationships.

One of the facts about commercial television which the Christian family may take most seriously has to do with the role of television in the moral formation of the person. In 1975 the Administrative Board of the U. S. Catholic Conference published a document on television and family life. In this document is found the following statement: "In our society today, television is the single most formative influence in shaping people's attitudes and values." Words to give the Christian parent pause.

The values and attitudes proclaimed by commercial television can be summarized in one statement: The good life depends on the unlimited acquisition of personal possessions. What you own is more important than what you are. Appearances matter more than reality. You should be willing to do anything you can get away with to become as affluent as possible. (In other words, that business about the camel and the eye of a needle is a lot of foolishness.)

There are families who have decided that life is more sane and human with no television at all. Others limit television watching to one hour a day, with exceptions now and then for special programs. After the initial "withdrawal" period, the children in such families invariably decide that life with little or no television is quite a good life.

Christian family members may find themselves asking in all seriousness if there are not better ways to be well-informed than watching television—reading newspapers, books, and magazines, for example. They may decide that there are forms of entertainment which are far more beneficial, on both the personal and family levels. A family can gain far more from a leisurely walk around the block together than it will from thirty minutes of group television watching.

A Christian family spirituality may also be sensitive to issues of peace and justice and to ways in which the family can have a positive impact on society at large. The family may become aware of the injustices which continue to exist due to racism. They may or may not join picket lines, but they can make efforts to sensitize both children and parents to the equality of all races and the consequences of both personal and institutional forms of racism.

Art and decorations in the home can be used to reflect various races and their cultures. Children, especially when they are very young, can be exposed to music from other cultures by means of recordings from a public library. It is a simple matter, also, to subscribe to a magazine or two which feature photographs of various racial groups. Parents can be sensitive to racial stereotypes in children's books and be prepared to counter these. Of course, many families are fortunate enough to live in cities where several races mix to make up the population. In such places, there are many opportunities to learn an appreciation for racial and ethnic values, if the family decides to involve itself at the right times in the right places.

Sexism is another justice issue which the family may strive to counteract. By distributing household chores with no regard for what is traditionally "men's work" and "women's work," the Christian family can form children and adults who are better prepared to oppose sexism in both society and the church. If children see that Mom and Dad treat one another as equals—that Mom takes out the garbage about as often as Dad, and Dad cleans house, washes dishes, and does the laundry; if they see that Mom can change the oil in the car and has an important role to play in "bringing home the bacon" they will be less likely to be affected by sexism than many of their peers.

In the Christian family there may be less support for placing women "on a pedestal" in order to keep them "in their place." There may be some very interesting discussions around the family table as girls discover that in their parish church they are not allowed to be altar servers alongside their brothers, let alone ever consider ordination to the priesthood as a life's goal.

War and peace is another issue which may have significant impact on a Christian family spirituality. Many families have accepted with enthusiasm the U. S. bishops' invitation to fast from meat on Fridays as a way to pray for peace and an end to the nuclear arms race. This is but one way in which families can allow issues of war and peace to touch their life. Another is that parents may find themselves called upon to be supportive of teenage sons as they struggle with their feelings about draft registration.

Closely related to issues of war and peace is the

Christian thrust toward nonviolence in human relationships. By learning and making use of techniques for the
nonviolent resolution of family conflicts, a Christian
family may be better prepared to adopt a Christian
position on the place of nonviolence in national and international disputes.

Underlying the Christian family's interest and involvement in issues such as those mentioned here is the
conviction that citizenship is subordinate to faith, that
the Christian is called to observance of the gospel
before he or she is called to salute the flag. The Christian family understands perfectly well the famous
words of St. Thomas More: "The king's good servant,
but God's first."

The fact that it is a family which is involved in these
issues is of special significance. The symbolic value of
family involvement in peace and justice issues is never
to be underestimated. Although the idea receives more
lip service than serious attention, it remains true that
the family is the most basic building block of society.
When families begin to change their lifestyle and
become active on social issues, elected leaders pay attention. They are well aware that the next thing they
feel may be the shaking of the foundations.

Another way in which the Christian family may
become counter-cultural has to do with the cultivation
of quiet in the home. We live in a world made noisy by
technology: cars, motorcycles, jack hammers, television sets and radios, appliances that wash and dry,
gadgets that whir, roar, clatter, and ping.

It seems nearly impossible to manufacture a child's
mechanical toy without including a noise-maker of
some kind. Children learn from an early age that in

order to have a good time they must be making noise.

It is nearly normal for the American home to never be quiet, unless everyone is asleep—and sometimes not even then. (How many people fall asleep each night in front of a still active television set?) We feel a compulsion to turn on a radio to drive away the quiet in our homes and in our cars. Many housewives leave a television set on whether they are watching it or not. It is taken for granted by many parents that teenagers are constitutionally incapable of doing homework without the music of their subculture playing loudly in the same room.

Everywhere we go there is "background music," even in elevators, and even when some store or business puts us on "hold" on the telephone.

Some families have decided to regain some control over this dimension of their life, to build in a bit of quiet in the family environment. A few simple rules can make an enormous difference. One family decided that, as a general rule, when there are two or more people in the family car at the same time, the radio will not be turned-on. They now find that more talking happens on both short and long trips in the car.

This same family decided to accept the rule that no music is allowed while doing homework. Not so remarkably, a positive effect has been noticed on the quality of schoolwork being done and on the grades being brought home.

Another family has set 9:00 p.m. as the hour when, on weekdays, all noise makers must be turned off. No television, no music, no blender in the kitchen going whir-grind-whir. At a family meeting, all agreed that this was a good decision. Each family member could tell of ways in which the quiet has been good for him or her.

Another family, which belongs to a religious tradition known to be "outside the mainstream," simply owns none of the domestic "conveniences" like television sets, radios, and power lawn mowers. Their home strikes the visitor like an island of quiet in an ocean of noise. Though this family's beliefs about cultivating quiet may strike most as extreme, there is no arguing with the obvious fact that the children in this home are more calm, more quiet, than the typical ten- and twelve-year-old.

The various traditional spiritualities which have developed over the centuries all agree on this point—that quiet and stillness are necessary to the spiritual, physical, and emotional health of the person. It is of value, if nothing else, to be able to hear oneself think now and then. A Christian family may feel a need to take some steps toward making life a bit more quiet, especially in the family environment of the home. To do so, of course, is counter-cultural in a world which swims in noise like a fish swims in water. At the same time, however this may be one of the more manageable ways in which the Christian family can allow its lifestyle to be shaped by an "in but not of the world" sprituality. All it takes is the decision to do it.

When families decide to take charge of their life—to take back some of the control over their life which has unwittingly and gradually been turned over to influences outside the family circle; when families begin to reclaim the power to shape their own values and pass along to children a living religious tradition in place of the gods of the dominant culture, society can't help but be affected.

Families have the power to change the world. One important aspect of a family spirituality is the challenge presented to families to take one giant step forward, and do just that.

Chapter 10

THE FAMILY PROCLAIMS THE GOOD NEWS

IN his Apostolic Exhortation, *On Evangelization in the Modern World,* Paul VI noted that all the objectives of the Second Vatican Council "are definitively summed up in this single one: to make the church of the twentieth century ever better fitted for proclaiming the gospel to the people of the twentieth century."

The domestic church/family is in an especially good position to play an effective part in this mission of proclaiming the gospel in ways that are credible in today's world. For the ideals and values upon which the family is founded are precisely the ideals and values for which so many people long.

We live in a world which hungers for human intimacy and intimacy with the divine. In its own unique ways, yet in ways it shares with all of human history, our age gives witness to the timeless words of St. Augustine: "Our hearts are restless until they rest in thee."

The Christian family strives to live according to the spirit of the gospel in the everyday world. By doing this it proclaims that the meaning of life is to be found in a human intimacy which is experienced as inseparable from intimacy with God.

Even the most obvious aspects of the dominant consumer culture in our society reflect a fascination with and hunger for all that "family" represents. The language and images of family and of human intimacy may be second only to sex in their power to sell things.

The word "family" is used in the advertising campaigns of restaurants, photographers' studios, automobile dealerships, travel agencies, and theaters, to name but a few examples. There is something about calling a restaurant a "family" restaurant that appeals to people. One auto dealership put up huge, expensive, lighted signs to announce to one and all that its showroom was not a showroom after all. It had become a "family room"!

Banks and insurance companies are especially adept at the use of human intimacy language to sell their services. Their advertising invariably includes words like these: trust, fidelity, caring, protection, friend. One bank calls itself "the friend of the family." "Like a good neighbor," a well known insurance company "is there."

The psychology behind the use of family and human intimacy language for commercial purposes is not difficult to discover. It is easy to imagine the voice of an advertising executive: "People want family, they crave close, warm human relationships, right? But they aren't getting them. Look at the divorce rate; look at how people don't trust one another anymore. Parents and kids are strangers to one another. People don't even know their next-door neighbors! So what we do is capitalize on people's desire for family and human relationships. We use the language of family and friendship to *sell*! We promise 'em warm family relationships if they buy a car or eat in a restaurant. We use images of people who really *like* one another to sell soft drinks and beer."

The fact is that if this tactic didn't actually work, billions of dollars would not be spent each year to produce advertising of precisely this nature. We are at-

tracted to cars, restaurants, and home video games by
the suggestion that they will bring family unity and
friendship into our life.

What this illustrates is simply that people today do
have a deep desire for human relationships that are
more than superficial. Ultimately what we all long for
is the loving God who alone can satisfy the thirst for the
Infinite with which we are created. This is why the ordinary Christian family can be such a powerful agent in
the proclamation of the gospel. Through its life
together the family gives witness to the fulfillment to be
found by those who base all of life on the building of
human intimacy and intimacy with God. This is what
the Christian family/domestic church is about. The
Christian family becomes an agent of evangelization by
being what it is: the smallest gathering of the friends
and followers of Christ.

Elaborate evangelization programs may be developed
on the international and national levels. The day may
come when Catholic evangelization agencies with
budgets in the hundreds of thousands of dollars produce highly sophisticated programs for broadcast over
cable television channels. Someday such television pro-
ductions may be bouncing from one orbiting satellite to
another twenty-four hours a day. Such agencies may
produce movies for circulation to theaters all over the
world. But helpful as all this may turn out to be,
nothing will ever match the importance and effectiveness of ordinary Christian families as they do their
best to be small cells of Christian life. All the talk and all
the "Christian-oriented entertainment" in the world
can never match the potential impact of families who
act on their convictions, who really strive to live their
faith.

It remains true that "actions speak louder than words." As Paul VI said, "The first means of evangelization is the witness of an authentically Christian life, given over to God in a communion that nothing should destroy and at the same time given to one's neighbor with limitless zeal."

The Christian family embodies a kind of paradigmatic response to the command of Christ to love God and neighbor. Thus, the spirit and lifestyle of the family calls others by means of its simple witness to find life's meaning through a similar dedication to love of God and other people.

The purpose of evangelization, according to Paul VI, is first of all to invite others to conversion of heart. The domestic church/family does this most effectively by the witness of its daily life. For the ideal toward which the Christian family strives is to order its entire existence according to this central thrust of the gospel. Though each family will do so "according to its lights" and according to its unique talents and character, the governing principle remains that of allowing the spirit of Christ to shine forth in all things.

Again, Paul VI: "Through this wordless witness these Christians stir up irresistible questions in the hearts of those who see how they live: Why are they like this? Why do they live in this way? What or who is it that inspires them? Why are they in our midst? Such a witness is already a silent proclamation of the Good News and a very powerful and effective one."

By placing the family first, by setting aside regular times to nourish marital and family relationships, the domestic church/family proclaims the gospel. By serving one another and by a dedication to serving others with special needs, the family evangelizes. By its dedication to ordinary family prayer and ritual the family gives witness to the presence of Christ in its midst. By commitment to a local parish community the family proclaims that social and spiritual unity with others is vital to the living of the gospel. And by its efforts to be guided by the spirit of Christ rather than by the spirit of a merely secular culture, the family indicates to others that only through the love of God and neighbors do the pieces of the puzzle that is human existence take on any semblance of order.

But Paul VI points out that evangelization, if it is to be complete, will also take the form of words: "The Good News proclaimed by the witness of life sooner or later has to be proclaimed by the word of life."

What does this mean for a Christian family? That families ought to find ways to "corner" others and talk to them about the gospel? That families should go knocking on strangers' doors in an attempt to gain entry to their homes and talk about Christ? On the contrary, the last thing this means is that families should look for ways to "get pushy for Jesus." This approach is customary with certain fundamentalist sects, but it is alien to the perspectives of Catholicism, as well as being alien to the spirit of virtually all of the mainline Protestant churches.

Again, Paul VI provides wise guidance: "The church is an evangelizer, but she begins by evangelizing herself." The domestic church/family evangelizes itself first. This is one reason for the importance of all that has been discussed in this book so far. As a family we act on our beliefs because we want our faith to shape our whole life, not just our words and our Sunday mornings. In the process, we say to ourselves over and over that we are disciples of Christ. In a very real sense, we proclaim the gospel to ourselves as we attempt to respond to the promptings of the Spirit.

There is another dimension of this self-evangelization. By our efforts to live the gospel we reinforce in our own mind and heart an identity we have adopted, one which makes us different from many others. The Christian family views life and the world in ways that differ, sometimes considerably, from the perspectives of a secular culture. And so we encourage one another and "build one another up" by means of the self-evangelization aspects of our Christian family lifestyle and spirituality.

Parents find themselves with a special role to play in the evangelization that goes on within the family. For parents remain at all times during their children's growing-up years their most influential and effective catechists. Parents have heard for a good number of years now that they are the primary religious educators of their children. But many still struggle with the everyday implications of this truth.

The kinds of catechesis that happen within the family are not only the most important from the perspective of the child's need for ongoing formation in the Christian life. Catechesis includes evangelization, that is, a way of sharing with the child the basic message of the gospel. This is where it becomes important for parents to feel comfortable with verbalizing their faith. Some Catholic parents may find it necessary to overcome a reluctance to talk about their life experience from a faith perspective. They may have inerited this reticence from their own family of origin. Parental actions remain more important than words, but actions without verbal commentary may not have as great an impact on the child as will a combination of the two.

Paul VI: "In the long run, is there any other way of handing on the gospel than by transmitting to another person one's personal experience of faith?" This is one challenge which confronts many Catholic parents today. Yet this verbalizing of parental faith is not to be understood so much as a matter of formal "discussions about religion." This may happen now and then, but what matters most is that the parent be able to include the religious dimension of existence in his or her conversations with the child from the earliest days of life through to adulthood.

The two-year-old is fascinated with an insect as it crawls up the side of a tree. The on-the-ball parent may simply include in his or her sharing of the child's excitement a comment about how wonderful our good God must be to be able to make such a big tree and such a tiny bug.

The ten-year-old is awe-struck by a spectacular lightning storm or is anxious about his or her own parents' marriage upon hearing of the divorce of a schoolmate's parents. These are opportunities for "God-talk," natural times when the sacred can be acknowledged and invoked in genuine, nonpietistic ways—ways that simply include the sphere of the sacred in the conversation.

The teenager asks serious religious questions. The wise parent may simply join the budding adult in asking the same questions, in admitting the same doubts. This is a time for simply reassuring the teenager that we are with him or her on the sometimes confusing paths of his or her search. Ready-made answers may hurt more than they help.

The parent who would be an effective evangelizer of his or her offspring is the one who resists the temptation to act as if responsibility for this aspect of parenting can be turned over to a Catholic school or parish religious education program. Seductive though this temptation may be, the realistic parent knows that it is a fool's dream, that it cannot be done, that the greatest impact on the child's religious development *will* happen—for good or for ill—within the context of family relationships. Such parents expect no more than supplemental help from schools and CCD programs. They then do what they can to understand faith on an adult level and to gain the fundamental knowledge and skills needed to incorporate faith and a Christian perspective into the normal events of family life.

Yet evangelization and catechesis within the family is by no means a one-way street. Paul VI again: "The parents not only communicate the gospel to their children, but from their children they can themselves receive the same gospel as deeply lived by them." Even the youngest child can provide parents with new insights into the Divine Mystery or the meaning of the gospel. By reflecting on their own best moments with their children parents learn more about how God "feels" and "acts" in relationship to them. When parents stand back and let the toddler learn to walk by falling and getting up to try again, they learn that this is how God is with them, too. Often the best parental behavior reflects beautifully the nature of God's relationship to the parent.

Even the most ordinary behavior of a child can teach parents more about the meaning of Jesus' words that we must become like a child if we would enter the kingdom of heaven. Words of Martin Luther illustrate

in-depth some words from the Sermon on the Mount:
"Do as your children do. They go to bed at night and
sleep without worries. They don't care whence they
will get soup or bread tomorrow; they know that Father
and Mother will take care of it."

Parents are very effectively evangelized by their
children, if they are open to this. They can gain many
insights into the meaning of the old adage, "Act as if
you had faith and faith will be given to you."

Yet the need to add words to evangelizing actions
also finds expression outside the immediate family, in
the community at large. Families that strive to allow the
gospel to shape their life from the ground up tend to
find themselves in situations where they can give
public witness to their faith. One family was invited to
participate in a city-wide forum on family life in the
modern world. In the course of their participation they
were able to speak of the fundamental place of Christian faith in their family relationships and of its impact
on their priorities and values.

Another family took part in an out-reach effort
organized by their parish which was designed to extend an open invitation to "un-churched" members of
their neighborhood to consider Catholicism. They did,
in fact, knock on doors, introduce themselves and give
to people an attractively printed leaflet on Catholicism
and their parish community. Far from an attempt to
"get pushy for Jesus," this evangelization effort was
fashioned to extend a warm invitation to other families
to consider the Catholic Christian way of life, if they
did not alredy belong to a church community.

Evangelization does not mean the effort to prosely-
tize or twist the arms of those who, with hardened

hearts, resist the grace of God. Instead, it means above all actually trying to live what we say we believe—that love of God and other people is what life is all about. In a secondary sense, it means following up with words when the opportuntiy arises, both within the family and in situations outside the family circle. Evangelization means making a statement that the God who is love dwells among his people, that this God can be trusted absolutely to care for us, and that therefore we are to turn our hearts away from, for example, the idols of the marketplace, in order to care for and love one another.

The Christian family/domestic church is in a prime position to proclaim precisely this gospel in the modern world.

AFTERWORD

ONE of the major themes of the gospel according to Matthew appears in these words of Matthew's Jesus: "None of those who cry out 'Lord, Lord,' will enter the kingdom of God but only the one who does the will of my Father in heaven" (7:21).

There is a constant temptation, in our time as in all times, to act as if religion has little to do with reality. Thus the common inclination to live as if baptism and the profession of a religious creed are meant to have only peripheral impact on our life as a family. There is the tendency to limit faith to words, to allow faith to dictate actions mainly on Sunday mornings and at times when the consequences of doing so will have little noticeable effect on the fabric of our life "in the real world" and in our home.

A family spirituality first conditions the "being" of the family; it is more about what the family *is*, than about what the family *does*. A family spirituality involves a simple, lived dedication to Christ in the real world. It is about prayer, faith, serving others, and so forth, of course. But because it is about such, it is also about laughter, about being foolish in the eyes of "the world," and about a great affection for a good party.

The spirituality for families suggested in these pages inspires us to say yes at times, no at others. It means we embrace the world with love and compassion, but we also call a spade a spade. Because of our family spirituality we share life and faith together but in ways which are always changing as both offspring and parents grow older, as the calendar pages fall and new ways of being family are needed. The spirituality we share also prompts us to nourish one another as individuals, to encourage individual action and growth.

A family spirituality is one that is in-process, undergoing transformation even as it transforms us and the life we share. As a family, we are not the same now as we were last year—or last month—and neither is our spirituality, our continuing efforts to follow the lead of the gospel in ways that make sense for our time and our place.

It must also be said, however, that the topic of "family spirituality" is, in large measure, unexplored territory. Families of all kinds are scouting out the terrain, learning from both their successful and unsuccessful efforts. In this they are either helped or handicapped by the kind of parish community to which they belong. An awesome responsibility rests with parish leaders today to support families in order to nourish the roots of the church.

An authentic Christian spirituality for families makes of the family what tradition teaches it is meant to be—"the first form of the church on earth" (Leo XIII), and a school of the Christian life. It is this family kind of spirituality which brings us home, to one another and to God.

SUGGESTIONS FOR FURTHER READING

Family Life in General
TRAITS OF A HEALTHY FAMILY, by Dolores Curran (Winston Press, 1983). "Must" reading for parents; excellent on virtually every aspect of practical family living. Ideal "spiritual reading" for anyone with family interests.

THE YOUNG CATHOLIC FAMILY, by Andrew M. Greeley (Thomas More Press, 1980). A sociological report which concludes that the strength of the church is to be found in the deep faith of young families and the passionate love of young spouses for one another.

Marriage as a Sacrament
CHRISTIAN MARRIAGE: A JOURNEY TOGETHER, by David M. Thomas (Michael Glazier, Inc., 1983). Perhaps the best development of a theology of marriage to appear since the Second Vatican Council. Written in language easily accessible to the educated adult.

MARITAL INTIMACY: A CATHOLIC PERSPECTIVE, by Joan Meyer Anzia and Mary G. Durkin (Loyola University Press, 1983). Reflections on the stages and phases of marriage, and a discussion of the place of sexuality in a marital spirituality.

MARRIAGE: SACRAMENT OF HOPE AND CHALLENGE, by William P. Roberts (St. Anthony Messenger Press, 1983). One of the best of a new breed of book on what constitutes the authentic religious nature of marriage as a total relationship. Avoids the pitfall of isolating the sacramental character of marriage to explicitly religious times.

Family Prayer and Ritual

FAMILY PRAYER, by Dolores Curran (St. Anthony Messenger Press, 1983). An outstanding up-date of an earlier book. One of the most realistic and practical books on the topic.

PRAYERS FOR THE DOMESTIC CHURCH, by Edward Hays (Forest of Peace Books, 1983). A beautiful collection of prayers and rituals for virtually every occasion, with informative introductory sections.

FAMILY NIGHTS THROUGHOUT THE YEAR, by Terry and Mimi Reilly (Abbey Press, 1982). An excellent resource for designing a weekly Family Night.

Sexuality

A JOYFUL MEETING: SEXUALITY IN MARRIAGE, by Drs. Mike annd Joyce Grace (International Marriage Encounter, 1980). One of the best books around on the differences between male and female and the impact of these differences on the sexual love of husband and wife.

THE MYSTERY OF SEXUALITY, by Rosemary Haughton (Paulist Press, 1972). Reflections on the various dimensions of human sexuality, their place in human development, spirituality, and interpersonal relationships.

Parenting and Religious Education

PASS IT ON, by James M. Ewens, S.J. (Arena Lettres, 1975). A practical resource for parents on how to pass along faith experiences in a family context.

BRINGING UP CHILDREN IN THE CHRISTIAN FAITH, by John H. Westerhoff III (Winston Press, 1980). Another "must" book. The author discusses parental roles in the religious education of children from the earliest years through adolescence. There is more wisdom and joy packed into this little book than in many books ten times its size.

THE SEARCH FOR AMERICA'S FAITH, by George Gallup, Jr. and David Poling (Abingdon Press, 1980). The impact of religious life on children and families plays a central role in this book by a prominent pollster and his associate. Excellent reading for parents who want to stay in touch with the real world in which their children are growing up.

Families and Social Justice

PEACEMAKING: FAMILY ACTIVITIES FOR JUSTICE AND PEACE, by Jacqueline Haessly (Paulist Press, 1980). Practical ideas for modifying competititve games to more cooperative models.

PARENTING FOR PEACE AND JUSTICE, by Kathleen and James McGinnis (Oribis, 1981). Excellent book, loaded with ideas that are rooted in family experience.

HOMEMADE SOCIAL JUSTICE, by Michael True (Fides/Claretian, 1982). A very readable "invocation" of the spirit of social justice as lived by families.

Roles in Marriage

DELIVERING THE MALE: OUT OF THE TOUGH GUY TRAP INTO A BETTER MARRIAGE, by Clayton C. Barbeau (Winston Press, 1982). How to overcome the straight-jacket aspects of the traditional male role in marriage. A great "examination of conscience" book for men, married or not.

THE SECOND STAGE, by Betty Friedan (Summit

Books, 1981). Very good for stimulating reflection on the husband-wife relationship and the place of work and parenting in family life; by one of the "founding mothers" of modern feminism.

SPIRITUAL PARTNERS: PROFILES IN CREATIVE MARRIAGE, by Cornelia Jessey and Irving Sussman (Crossroad, 1982). Stories of the marriages of several famous married couples, including Gilbert and Frances Chesterton, and Frank Sheed and Maisie Ward.

Family and Lifestyle

FOLLOWING CHRIST IN A CONSUMER SOCIETY, by John Francis Kavanaugh (Orbis, 1979). Examines the impact of faith on everyday lifestyle issues. An excellent, inspiring book.

THE PLUG-IN DRUG: CHILDREN, TELEVISION AND THE FAMILY, by Marie Winn (Bantam Books, 1978). Challenges popular attitudes concerning the impact of television on child development and the quality of family relationships. "Required reading" for parents.

Solitude and Family Life

THOUGHTS IN SOLITUDE, by Thomas Merton (Farrar, Straus & Giroux, 1958). For those who want to know more about the need for solitude in the modern world, there is nothing quite as good as this little classic.